OKLAHOMA CITY BOMBING
The Suppressed Truth

by

JON RAPPOPORT

The Book Tree
Escondido, California

First printing 1995

Second printing 1997

Copyright 1995 by Jon Rappoport

All rights reserved. No part of this publication may be reproduced or transmitted in any form or by any means, electronic or mechanical, including photocopy, recording, or any information storage and retrieval system, without permission in writing from the publisher.

ISBN 1-885395-22-1

Published by
The Book Tree
c/o P.O. Box 724
Escondido, California 92033

Trials are strange creatures. You think that justice will appear, finally, like a sword in the fire. You think a clarity will fill the sky. But who is presenting the real evidence?

Know that you are looking at a cover-up that began on the morning of April 19th, just after the Federal Building bombing, and continues to this day. Know that. Don't let them frog-march you into Oblivion.

If for any reason McVeigh does not come to trial, if he does not survive, realize that one more murder has taken place in Oklahoma.

Citizens believe that political truth is something you speak. Governments command that truth is something you bury with lies.

THE FIRST IMAGE

Shortly after nine o' clock on the morning of April 19th, 1995, an explosion hit the Murrah Federal Building in Oklahoma City.
In the wake of great human devastation, that same day, FBI agents found a VIN (vehicle ID number) in the rubble. They determined they were looking for a 1993 Ford truck owned by Ryder. Ryder in Miami said the truck was at a rental company, Elliot's Body Shop, in Junction City, Kansas.
Still on April 19th, the rental agent at Elliot's told the FBI that two people had rented that truck on April 17. The man who signed for the truck was Bob Kling. The name turned out to be a fake.
On April 20th, FBI agents went back to Elliot's. Two artist's sketches of the men who rented the Ryder truck were made.
Three witnesses who had been at the Federal Building in OK City, just before the bomb went off, made a positive ID on one of the drawings, called Unsub #1.
The FBI took copies of the artist's sketches and interviewed people in Junction City. Several employees of the Dreamland Motel recognized Unsub #1. They looked in their registry and found the name Tim McVeigh. McVeigh had stayed at Dreamland from the 14th of April through the 18th. McVeigh had signed in with a Michigan address. North Van Dyke Road, Decker, Michigan.
The Michigan DMV located a license for Timothy

J. McVeigh. Address, 3616 North Van Dyke Road, Decker. That address turned out to be a farm. The FBI discovered two names vis-a-vis the farm: Terry Nichols and James Nichols.

A relative of James Nichols said McVeigh was a friend of James, and James had worked at the farm on North Van Dyke. The relative also mentioned hearing that James Nichols had a sizeable amount of fertilizer and fuel oil, and had constructed bombs with them in the past.

On April 21, a man who used to work with McVeigh called the FBI. He had just seen the artist's Unsub #1 sketch on TV. He said McVeigh was a right-winger, had been in the Army, and had at one point gone to Waco to look at the ruins of the Branch Davidian compound. McVeigh, he said, was very upset about what had happened there, what the federal agents had done.

This man gave the FBI an address. 1711 Stockton Hill Road, Kingman, Arizona.

The same day, April 21, the FBI learned McVeigh had already been arrested in Perry, Oklahoma, for no license plate and for carrying a concealed weapon. That arrest occurred only an hour and a half after the blast at the Federal Building in Oklahoma City. During booking, McVeigh had written down James Nichols as a reference.

Federal agents picked up McVeigh and charged him with blowing up the Federal Building.

Charles Hangar, the Oklahoma State Trooper who originally stopped McVeigh for driving with no plate, states that McVeigh told him he had a weapon--after Hangar noticed a bulge under the jacket on the left side and ordered McVeigh to pull back the jacket. The weapon was a loaded 45-caliber Glock, model 21, SER-VW769.

All of the above information is derived from the FBI McVeigh-arrest warrant, issued on April 21, 1995, and Oklahoma State Trooper Hangar's affidavit. What lies beyond these official documents is something else again.

THE SECOND IMAGE

We sit down across from each other in a booth, in a coffee shop in North Hollywood.

He says, "There'll be media people who agree with you. But you probably won't hear about them. They'll be isolated."

"Meaning who?"

"A few reporters in Oklahoma City."

"They're mad?"

"Very. A TV guy who's put in twelve years. He's tired of looking at junk float across his desk. He's blowing his stack. He wants some answers."

"I haven't heard about any of this."

"That's what I mean. They keep it local. The network in New York kills it. Lets it fester in Oklahoma City."

"But this guy definitely doesn't believe the government scenario."

"Definitely not. He thinks the federal government...some part of it, knew the bombing was coming two months before it happened."

"Sounds like that New York Times article a couple of years ago. What was his name?"

"The undercover FBI guy? Salem. Emad Salem."

"He taped conversations with other agents. Showed the FBI knew the Trade Center was going to be blown up."

"Not only that. He said he was going to put some kind of phony powder into the bomb, to make it inert, but his supervisor told him not to."

"And what happened to that story? Vanished into thin air."

We talked a little while longer, he got up, bought himself a lottery ticket and walked out the door.

Just another conversation between two reporters...

No names at first. Nobody wants to give me his name. Off the record only. But I don't care. I'm already into strange territory, so I'll talk to anyone, even if he's a ghost.

The April 19th bombing of the Federal Building in Oklahoma City is given one media-twist: It was the work of amateurs.

The portrait is sketched in of two or three wackos who were super-patriots, obsessed with Waco and in need of causing violence...weird rednecks who were connected to larger militias run by other rednecks.

These wackos did a crazy thing. They rented a 24-foot Ryder truck that anybody could trace...because they were stupid, and they bought 4800 pounds of fertilizer, which anybody could trace...because they were stupid rednecks, and they drove the truck up to the Fed Bldg. and set off a bomb.

End of scenario.

Now think this through with me. Follow this. These stupid ex-soldiers blew up the building, and then McVeigh drove off in a car without a license plate,

and he was stopped by a cop an hour and a half later. The cop said, "Hmm, this guy's driving without a plate, I think I'll cite him." The cop does. Only as he's about to let McVeigh go, he notices a distinct bulge under McVeigh's windbreaker. He says: "What's that?"
McVeigh says, "Officer, I have a weapon under here."
Gingerly, McVeigh, who's just killed over a hundred federal employees, and knows that this arrest could end his life outside jail or outside the electric chair, gingerly McVeigh opens his jacket and reveals a 9mm Glock pistol. Also a five-inch knife hanging from his belt.
"Hmm," the officer says. He puts his service revolver to McVeigh's head and takes him to jail in nearby Perry. On ice for three days, McVeigh is then picked up by the feds and guided right into custody as the bomber. Good work, men.
Why does a killer of a hundred sixty-eight people balk at killing a cop with a Glock pistol on a lonely highway to avoid being arrested? Stupid redneck, stupid misguided Patriot wackos. That's the reason. That's all we need to know.
Except it turns out that the explosion was not stupid, it was extremely vicious.

The explosion is the key. The fertilizer, ammonium nitrate, is mixed with fuel oil to make a slurry, called ANFO, and that slurry is sitting in twenty plastic containers in the Ryder truck parked next to the curb at the Federal Bldg. Each one of the containers has in it 240 pounds of mixture. There is one detonator, the government says, one long cord, called a det cord. It is very, very flammable. A flame shoots along it at high speed. So maybe the det cord is threaded through all the plastic containers, and then you get, supposedly, a simultaneous explosion of all the ANFO. Simultaneity gives you one shock wave.

Because ONE COHERENT SHOCK WAVE has to happen or the explosion is weak. That kind of coordinated precision theoretically asks for 20 detonators, all timed to the exact same instant, hooked to all the plastic containers in the truck. Required: one highly experienced pro.

Or, using that very flammable det cord, you make a SPECIFIC careful ring pattern, by the book, including all the plastic containers, and you go for simultaneity. But that ring-pattern can't be done by somebody who doesn't know his butt from his elbow. It also has to be done by a pro. You can't just lead the det cord through all the containers like a snake and hope a contagion spreads as the ignition occurs. That won't work. Explosives experts verify this.

I won't describe the exact method necessary, but it requires perfectly cut lengths of det cord, and so on.

So yes, a det cord can work, but it isn't easy, and it isn't always reliable. A stupid redneck who gets arrested with no license plate seems like a very unlikely prospect.

There's another, more serious absurdity. The one thing you eliminate with ammonium nitrate, to make it explode well, is AIRSPACE, regardless of how well it's connected up with det cord. Anybody who works with the stuff knows that. You pour it in ONE container and then there is no air between the particles of the explosive. Or you pour it down a structural column and fill it up. But twenty plastic containers in a truck? There's nothing BUT airspace between the containers. That's death for a coherent explosion. Especially with plastic as the material of the containers. With all that airspace in the truck, you may get no explosion. Or you could wind up with a partial ignition, and fertilizer all over the city.

So the whole ammonium nitrate setup in the truck, as the government describes it, and the media describe it, is a very dumb way of doing things. Very unlikely way of causing damage.

Except for that one thing. A quarter of the building went down. A hundred sixty-eight people were tragically killed and six hundred were injured. Did this stupid redneck manage to do a very unredneck kind of thing?

To any half-conscious reporter, this would signal a problem. Things don't fit. The bomb, which was, as described by investigators, a foolish affair, put together by an obvious amateur, accomplishes a horrendous objective that requires, apparently, a pro.

But the idea of a pro isn't part of the scenario in progress, isn't part of the instant cartoon reality being built for the public. McVeigh IS guilty. That's assumed. That's part of the deal. McVeigh IS dumb.

That's part of his image. After all, he bought traceable fertilizer and a traceable truck, and he drove around without a license and he told the arresting trooper he had a pistol under his windbreaker. This IS an amateur production. That's what the media is giving us. This is the created image.
Doesn't matter what is revealed later. First impressions count. They endure.
Needless to say, the government investigators play along. It's easier than it sounds. Most of the investigators have learned, through experience, that the basic IMPOSED scenario is the structure they HAVE TO work with. They know they have to operate inside the picture frame devised by others. The remainder of the federal police are doubters who keep their doubts to themselves, because their jobs are riding on the line.

So, with the contradictions implicit in the ammonium nitrate scenario, already there is a big problem. This alone should be sufficient to cause a stir. If you found out nothing else but THIS, you could make a case that the fed investigation is way off the mark and probably a phony procedure. A fantasy-trip. Because, presumably, the FBI has a few bomb experts who can see the deficiencies in its own interpretation of the explosion.

A reporter in OK City found one credible witness to the blast. This witness said that the Fed Bldg. collapsed in on itself, like a demolition. In that case, we would not be dealing with a shock wave launched out of a rental truck. We would be confronted with a rumbling commercial-type implosion, which we've all seen a hundred times on TV. The building grumbles, yawns, and falls straight down.

In fact, from the examination of the pancaking effect of the collapse, that is what appears to have happened. From the beginning, observers who know how explosives work questioned the truck-bomb as the true source of the major decimation. Why? Because an ANFO bomb out of a truck creates a circular pattern of destruction. A spherical pattern. And, looking at photos of the building after the blast, people saw a linear, left to right pattern. There were serious doubts right away.

How do you get a quarter of a building to fall down from the top, to collapse in on itself? You set shaped charges inside the building at certain points on the structural supports. That's how. It's a precise piece of work.

How many bomb experts have you seen questioned VERY carefully on TV? None?

I spoke with a producer at ABC. I gave him all this information, and more, concerning the explosion. He was interested. Finally he said, "Keep me posted on what you find out."

This is an ABC producer telling me that. He has

more resources at his fingertips in one day than I've had in fifteen years, and he wants ME to keep digging. No, sorry. If I were in his place, I'd leap at the chance to discredit the government scenario, even if I didn't have all the answers in a neat package. I mean, isn't that a titillating headline: NEW LEAD IN OKLAHOMA BOMBING; GOVERNMENT STORY BORDERS ON SHEER INVENTION. But as both you and I know, that's a chuckle banner, an April Fool's fake, because editors at the top of the heap just don't do serious walk-abouts outside government-imposed realities. It's a big no-no.

The government is protected, even when it's trashed. It's all right to dig holes in official walls, but to imply that the whole edifice is rotting from within? Sorry. That only creeps in, as oblique speculation, after the fact, after the verdict has come down, after the ink is dry, after the emotions have cooled, after the trial, after McVeigh is serving life or is dead. You can count the exceptions to this rule on the fingers of one hand.

Now, if the building was taken out by an implosion, a demolition, then we would be talking, yes, pros at work. In which case, McVeigh, the amateur, assumes a whole new dimension.

He becomes the visible part of a sophisticated operation, in which the truck bomb was a diversion from the main event. He becomes the blameable man, the one we can find.

The choice as the fall-guy.

Just keep that possibility in mind.

Consider this as a scenario:

The pros needed a mind-scrambling diversion at the moment the building fell, so that witnesses on the street wouldn't realize the whole thing was a very familiar-looking demolition, caused by interior charges placed on the support columns. The obvious diversion would be the disorienting HUGE BANG out of the Ryder truck. A pro in a building across the street has a remote clicker in his hand. He sits at a window and looks down at the street. The instant the truck blows he presses a key and the building implodes and collapses. It's a piece of death-dealing stage magic.

McVeigh, the redneck, he's the throwaway. He's the man who was set up. He's the dupe.

Consider this as a maybe.

It all starts with the explosion. If it turns out that the Ryder truck setup couldn't have done the damage that occurred, you're in new territory. You've made a reality shift, and things have new meanings.

In the Oklahoma City case, we're certainly looking at an attempt to discredit the Patriots. One reason? Because somewhere between 35 and 300 counties in the US, influenced by dialogue with these Patriot-people, have passed resolutions declaring non-cooperation with the federal government. This is called the home-rule movement. It's essentially a split-off from the federal authorities in Washington. It means that counties are saying THEY are the prime unit of government. (See the LA Times, April 5/95, page 1. The story on Nye County, Nevada.)

This is big-time stuff. This is a startling way of expressing citizen-dissatisfaction with the federal government. It's much more corrosive than protests outside official buildings. The Department of Justice has now filed a suit against Nye County, Nevada, one of the prime movers in this expanding home-rule movement. The Justice Dept. is very worried. Nye County officials have stated that they consider all federal land in their jurisdiction to be property OF THE COUNTY, NOT THE FEDERAL GOVERNMENT. It so happens that in Nye, 93% of all land is federally owned. Nye's County Commissioner has personally smashed a barrier erected by the feds to stop county citizens from using a federal access-road into national forest territory. Residents want to use the national land for cattle grazing.

The home-rule movement basically states that a county can decide to what degree it wants to cooperate with federal officials...on ANY federal law or regulation that seems to be invasive and intrusive.

In addition, many Patriots state, over and over, that the IRS is an illegal institution, a collection agency for a private group called the Federal Reserve--which, they claim, is masquerading as a part of the government. Patriot researchers have combed older law, and cross-referenced one other's work in a multi-thousand hour loosely knit investigation, whose conclusions about the Fed Reserve and the IRS attract new people every day...people who are fed up with the Washington brand of governing.

The feds are terrified of all this. Are terrified of losing control. Are terrified of the idea that many, many Americans will stop paying income taxes.

Discrediting ALL Patriots has become a priority for Washington. An attempt is being made to do that now.

More on the explosion. (There's ALWAYS more on the explosion.) One bomb expert I talked to off the record told me, "From the power of the blast, I would expect that, if it came from the truck, the shock wave would have gone all the way through the back of the building. But it didn't."

Why aren't reporters asking about this?

I spoke with a writer for the Daily Oklahoman, the only paper in Oklahoma City. I asked her if the damage done across the street on the other side of the truck, away from the Federal Building, was considerable.

"Well," she said, "a lot of it was structural. Buildings are still standing, but they'll have to be taken down eventually."

"Was the amount of damage across the street what you'd expect, given what happened to the Federal

Building?"
"No," she said after a short pause. She didn't give me her last name. Intentionally didn't give it to me. Anyone could tell from the sound of her voice that she wasn't about to press this unequal damage pattern with her editor. Our conversation was in late April. Her paper, by July 1, has said nothing about this question.

McVeigh must be guilty. After all, as soon as he was taken into custody, Time Magazine put his crew-cut mug on the cover, with the caption, THE FACE OF TERROR. That magazine, the national home of faintly patronizing stories that go nowhere, written by reporters who believe that sources-not-official are just too, too tacky...this magazine, before the arrest papers are even dry, goes with THE FACE OF TERROR. Any employee with a few live brain cells and an even fragmentary conscience ought to throw down a resignation letter on the spot and walk out of that perfumed fun-house.

Could anything be more blatant? Trial before jury. Prosecution and verdict before trial. Let's just make the FBI judge and executioner. Hang the kid immediately in the town square.

The LA Times fell right into line. It began sending people out on the road to reconstruct McVeigh's last few months. Where he was, who he talked to, how he lived. How much of this "digging" was actually done at FBI offices and lunch counters with law enforcement officials is unknown. Point is, the question up for grabs was no longer, WHO DID IT? It was now, HOW DID HE DO IT? and WHY? To go back to that WHO question would be very expensive in terms of a reporter's career. If Tom Brokaw suddenly grew a third eye and decided he wanted to start all over at the beginning and look for the bomber, McVeigh or no McVeigh, Mr. Brokaw would now be doing weather in a public bathroom in Central Park.

THAT'S one of the essential facts to grasp. Reporting can't be done. It's off-limits. What you can do, if you hate right-wing bigots and/or people with guns is, you can go on the air and, a priori, tie in McVeigh with all of THEM and then make the lot of them GUILTY by acclaim. That you can get away with. You can say McVeigh was illiterate and it just proves the whole trouble with this country is that nobody READS anymore. You can say McVeigh was a monster raised by parents who were inbred and it happens all the time in the hills of the southern midwest or upstate New York, where the righteous can't see farther than Armageddon. You can say that. You can say we have to make the government pay more attention to the deprived, so that monsters like McVeigh aren't cultured in such obviously heinous surroundings...only by better social engineering will we avoid future Oklahoma Cities. You can say that.

But you can't say that McVeigh didn't set off the real blast that took the building down, and the government is clearly lying, or any variation of that. You can't go back to the first question, which is, WHO DID IT?

The construction of reality. Announce a conclusion, and then refuse to allow access to those who dispute it. Continue to confirm the conclusion in any way necessary, and make it part of the world, even if it is completely false. Fake it. Pretend.

The country is full of pundits who think they understand the anti-federal Patriot movement. In truth, these self-styled arbiters of opinion don't want to be left behind. They don't want to feel a new category of politics is coming into being from which they will be excluded. Therefore, they place EVERYTHING in the world of Patriot groups under the familiar rubric of rightwing fundamentalist lunatic skinhead neo-Nazi uneducated uncultured gun crazy racist KKK Cromagnons.

Within the militia and Patriot phenomenon, there ARE people who have had ties to racist groups. Who are building MORE racism and anti-semitism. Who talk out of both sides of their mouths. This is pretty apparent. In other parts of the Patriot movement, which is perhaps nearing two million people, racism is absent, and the single issue--regardless of whether you agree with the Patriot SOLUTIONS--the single issue is excessive power and corruption within the federal government. A government, by the way, which, in the recent past, has been the largest purveyor of racism in the land.

As I write this, I am looking over a remarkable, and apparently authentic, document titled National Security Council Memorandum 46, issued on March 16th, 1978--and its companion piece, the NSC Study on "Black Africa and the US Black Movement." Both these documents are labeled Secret. The second document is a response to the first, which calls for "[a]ppropriate steps to be taken inside and outside the country in order to inhibit any pressure by radical African leaders and organizations on the US black community for the latter to exert influence on the policy of the Administration toward Africa." The document-response to this White House call for action recommends that "special clandestine operations should be launched by the CIA to generate mistrust and hostility in American and world opinion against joint activity of the two forces [black African and black US political groups]; and to cause division among black African radical national groups and their leaders."

This document goes on to list a policy program, including actions to "preserve the present climate which inhibits the emergence from within the [US] black leadership of a person capable of exerting nationwide appeal."

The policy program also supports "actions designed to sharpen social stratification in the [US] black community, which would lead to the widening and perpetuation of the gap between successful educated blacks and the poor, giving rise to growing antagonism between different black groups and a weakening of the [black political] movement as a whole."

Other proposed steps include taking "every possible means through the AFL-CIO leaders to counteract the increasing influence of black labor organizations which function in all major unions," and "support[ing] the nomination at federal and local levels of loyal black public figures to elective offices, to government agencies and the court." In this case, of course, the word loyal implies an allegiance toward federal policies which help create a weak black political force in America.

I quote this document just to give a little perspective.

McVeigh was in Kingman, Arizona, before he showed up in Oklahoma City. He worked part-time in a hardware store loading boxes. Not a very high-powered job. Yet witnesses have told the FBI that he had wads of cash on him. Two, three thousand dollars at a time. And the bomb cost somewhere between two and five thousand dollars, depending on whose figures you accept.

Where did the cash come from?

Possible scenario: In one of the Patriot Groups, McVeigh meets a man who becomes his mentor. This man sees in McVeigh a potential for violence. The mentor encourages it by saying, "There's big work ahead to be done. Important work for your country, if you want to save it...you're needed. Are you willing to wait, to educate yourself, to hang in for awhile until the day comes?...Here's some cash for you. Keep it to yourself. There's more where that came from..." That sort of thing, over a period of months.

Finally, McVeigh and some of his buddies decide it's time to make a wild statement. That energy and desire are directed by the "Patriot" mentor who is, of course, an intelligence field-agent, possibly John Doe 2.

Consider that. Just consider it.

In the case of McVeigh, so much silence surrounds him. So little has been dug up about his life. On several magazine shows, friends of his mentioned that he claimed a microchip was implanted in his body while he was in the Army. Naturally, this evokes the response that the man is insane. Who else would say such a thing? He'd been watching too many science fiction movies. Like a villain in those movies, McVeigh isn't given background by the press. He is left for us to see as a monomaniac, a man who knew only hate and frustration, and when the moment arrived, lashed out. Other than that, he has no character. He is a cipher, a kid in the Army. This non-rendering, of course, enforces the image of the killer. A neutrality, barely sketched in.

During the Gulf War, George Bush's war, the battlefield press were managed to a degree unknown previously. They were herded into headquarters at great remove from the front. They were kept busy with dispatches and briefings from US military people, and they found themselves issued with fatigues, which of course made them happy. They watched video of smart bombs going down holes in buildings. Phones were right there. Computers and links were right there. It was pretty comfortable.

Only much, much later, when the fighting was all over, did the disputes arise as to body counts and the killing. Only later did it come out that three hundred thousand Iraqis were wiped out, and many of them children. Only then did it become clear that smart bombs weren't so smart, that there was a great deal of destruction fanning out from the pinpoint targets. We began to hear about many, many returning veterans from the Gulf who had mysterious debilitating illnesses and conditions, stemming in part from experimental drugs and vaccines they had been dosed with here in America, BEFORE shipping out. If you think that's a fairy tale, call Senator Jay Rockefeller's office and have them send you their Committee report, and the conclusions of the two medical investigators who uncovered the whole mess. Basically, several hundred thousand American veterans in the Gulf, under the auspices of the Department of Defense, and the FDA, were experimental subjects in a highly dangerous drug trial. It was carried on in secret. When many of these veterans, back in the states, showed up ill at VA hospitals, asking for help, their Army med files showed no indication that they had been given the experimental vaccines and pharmaceuticals at all. Docs at the VA thought they were dealing with a mass hallucination. Well, they would. In fact, the experimental dosing with unlicensed drugs was intentionally left out of these veterans' records.

By a year after the war, the whole Top Gun oh boy image of the Army was lying in ruins, a spent ad campaign.

"Hey, what are you keeping those posters around for? Get rid of them!"

Of course, by then, how sheepish some of the

showbiz celebrities must have been feeling who had said SUPPORT OUR BOYS. Some of the same celebrities who made trouble during Vietnam, railing against that war, were really juiced up for the Gulf. They weren't going to make a bad mistake again. They weren't going to take heat one more time and anger their agents and their families. So they kept saying, SUPPORT OUR BOYS, as if every kid over there were Tom Cruise or Val Kilmer. It was all Miller Time and high fives on aircraft carriers. Hypnosis par excellence. America was sold one more bill of goods. AND US VETERANS PAID THE PRICE WITH THEIR HEALTH.

Point is, what is happening in Oklahoma City is another Gulf War. Right now. June 22nd, 1995. Reporters are isolated from the battlefront. They have no access. The remainder of the building has been destroyed, cutting links to vital forensic evidence. McVeigh is on ice. His lawyer has nothing of substance to say. The FBI is spinning press releases. There is silence. SUPPORT OUR BOYS. Somehow, because federal employees were killed in the blast, this implies that the FBI has the story right. To challenge their interpretation would be to desecrate the dead. CERTAINLY. SUPPORT OUR BOYS. It's a beautiful con. It assumes that everyone involved in the investigation is on the ball and American and honest and honorable and smart...all the way, and don't you forget it. No mistakes here. Not a one.

THE THIRD IMAGE

"Sir, is the CIA a legal terrorist group in our midst?"
"OF COURSE NOT."
"Sorry. Had to ask."
Or how about this: "Sir, we are told that twenty containers of ammonium nitrate slurry in the truck won't go off well. We're told that there's too much air space."
"That's absurd."
"Why is it absurd?"
"Because it DID go off."
"But with how much force? There may have been other bombs inside the building."
"There weren't. We looked."
"Sorry. Had to ask."

What OK City reporter has a true record of who arrived first on the scene after the explosion and what may have been removed? What reporter has thought about how little would be left of a shaped charge inside the building after the blast?
"The federal boys went over that thing with a fine tooth comb, and I can tell you there's nothing there."

Splendid.
Meanwhile, Oklahoma State Representative Charles Key has said, several times, including once on July 5th to a researcher in OK City, and once to me on

July 10, that a tow missile was found in the Federal Building after the blast. Where have you seen that quote? Did the NY Times run it? Sorry. And Phil O' Halloran, a sharp free-lance reporter, has Bill Martin, head of PR for the Oklahoma City Police, on the record saying he believes workers found MERCURY FULMINATE in the Federal Building after the blast. Containers of mercury fulminate. That substance is extremely volatile. It is used in explosives. Have you heard that? Why is that not being reported?

More on the explosion.
The one witness down in Oklahoma City, Peter Schaffer, the man who supposedly saw the blast, saw the building collapse in on itself like an implosion, is now saying he saw nothing. The building was already down, he says, when he first came upon it. But Ann Defrange, the Daily Oklahoman reporter who interviewed him on April 19th, who was struck by his description, remembers quite clearly what she heard. She told me so in three separate phone conversations.

I spoke with Ray Brown, a geophysicist at the University of Oklahoma. Brown works for the Geological Survey there.
Ray Brown, of course, has pored over the seismograph evidence of the explosion on April 19th. Two shock waves, ten seconds apart. That's what the

record says. Even allowing for what Brown calls overlap of the first and second wave, which gives a bit of a distorted picture, we are "not talking about one explosion and then a follow-up echo or reverberation of the buildings in the area." No. The second shock wave was SLIGHTLY MORE INTENSE, Brown says.

"As far as I'm concerned," Brown tells me, "right now we are looking at two events. With the overlap factor, they might have been four or five seconds apart. But that's still a lot."
"Two explosions?"
"That's a possible implication."

Larry Potts is the FBI guy from Ruby Ridge, Idaho, where in 1992 fed agents, carrying out a search warrant on one Randy Weaver and his home, shot Randy Weaver's wife in the face and killed her as she was holding her ten-month-old baby in her arms. She bled to death on her front porch. Larry Potts is in charge of the investigation in OK City.

The Salt Lake Tribune, May 11/95. Larry Potts, in charge of the investigation for the FBI in OK City, was also a participant in designing the assault plan in Waco that ended in the deaths of 80 people at the Davidian Branch compound. He was the FBI headquarters' supervisor at Ruby Ridge, where

Weaver's wife was killed by FBI sniper fire. Deadly fire is allowed only in cases of self-defense. Eugene Glenn, head of the FBI Salt Lake office, has stated to the Justice Department that Potts was responsible at Ruby Ridge for ordering that deadly fire. Now Janet Reno, even though Glenn's charge is still warm, has promoted Potts to Deputy Director of the FBI, under Louis Freeh. What is this? A birthday present?

Associated Press--"Single Bomb Destroyed Building; Seismic Records Shake Murrah Multiple Bomb Theory." This is one of the more transparent pieces of hack-job PR I've seen in a long time. Somehow, when federal people demolished the rest of the Fed Building on May 23rd, they used the occasion to find several seismic spikes on read-out charts which, they say, prove that EVERY BOMB causes multiple spikes...and the conspiracy buffs' several-bomb theory falsely arose from THAT kind of mistake the first time on April 19th.

Meanwhile, a geophysicist named Ray Brown, at the U of Oklahoma, is telling me that what he's seen of this recent federal demolition data proves nothing to him. He still thinks the April 19th tragedy at the Fed building involved "separate events." In other words, at least two bombs. But the lounge-act who wrote the story for AP conveniently made it look like there was no dissension among scientists and people in the know. What is AP now, the major arm of the Press Secretary's office at the White House? Where is Dee Dee when we need her?

I spoke with Brig. General USAF (Ret.) Ben Partin. Partin has a considerable amount of experience with weapons design and testing. He recently wrote a six-page letter to a number of Congressmen about the explosion in OK City.

Partin tells me, unequivocally, that the pattern of destruction on the roof of the building matches the pattern of destruction at the bottom of the building. In other words, the collapse was the result of internal charges which caused a quarter of the building to fall down, straight down. Implosion. This confirms Peter Schaffer's eyewitness description, which he has now recanted.

In his very specific report to the Congresspeople, General Partin jumps right in: "I can say, with a high level of confidence, that the damage pattern on the reinforced concrete superstructure could not possibly have been attained from the single truck bomb without supplementing demolition charges at some of the reinforced column bases. The total incompatibility with a single truck bomb lies in the fact that either some of the columns collapsed that should not have collapsed or some of the columns are still standing that should have collapsed and did not."

Partin is not yet appearing on Nightline.

His letter to Congress, dated May 17, 1995, asks for a stay on the federal demolition of the remainder of the building. His request fell on deaf ears.

Partin writes, "A careful examination of the collapsed column bases would readily reveal a failure mode produced by a demolition charge. This evidence would be so critical, a separate and independent assessment should be made before a building demolition team destroys the evidence forever."

Of course, the federal boys brought down the remainder of the building on the casually announced premise that all the evidence had been squeezed out of their investigation, all the secrets had been given up. According to State Representative Charles Key, the collapsed columns were actually crushed by the feds. Pulverized.

Partin told me, "People don't understand how fast the force of a truck bomb would decay. By the time that shock wave gets back inside the building, it's dropped off tremendously."

Partin includes, in his letter, a diagram. It shows that, side to side, the Fed Building contained three rows of columns. There were eleven columns in each row. He said to me, "Do you see there, in the second row, the B row of eleven columns, column B3? That was taken out. Now if the truck bomb had done that, it would also have exerted enough force to take out the adjoining columns, B4 and B5. But B4 and B5 were left standing after the blast on April 19th. So B3 was not taken out by the truck bomb. It was destroyed by a demolition charge inside the building. That's really all you have to know. You can stop right there. That tells you that the incident on April 19th had to include explosives inside the building."

And, as I mentioned earlier, that gives us a whole different ballgame.

Two days later I speak with Partin again. I want to nail down the column damage to the building, partly because there is a rumor circulating that no columns were actually affected. That all the damage was torn-out walls, ceilings, and floors, as a result of some kind of explosive device in the truck. I personally found this rumor absurd. Partin gives me the numbers: If you were standing next to the Ryder truck at the curb, looking at the front (north) of the building, the whole row of columns going from left to right, the A row, the first row you would encounter, sustained very heavy damage. Column A1, at the northeast corner of the building, is still left standing, but then columns A2 through A8 were taken out. Columns A9, A10, and A11 were left standing. Column B3, behind A3, is also down. The rest of row B is up and all of row C is up.

Partin emphasizes that by the time you get to column A7, you can't be talking about a device in the truck doing that damage. Over that sixty feet of distance, the force of the explosion would have decayed too much. And to boot, A7 is a monster of a pillar, and so, regardless, "had to have been knocked out with a device placed on it."

"You'd be looking for demolition charges that were put across row A on the third floor," Partin says.

A reporter from the Daily Oklahoman confirms that Partin has the right facts about which columns went down and which didn't.

Charles Mankin, head of the Geologic Survey at the University of Oklahoma, is, especially for a university employee, quite candid. I'm rather amazed he isn't dissembling and ducking and jabbing all over the place. I guess I'm used to folks further north, who

take every interview as a major piece of PR.
Mankin tells me, first, that, yes, there was considerable column damage to the building. "Columns on the east side were shattered badly. There is exposure all the way into the rebars."
Rebars are interior steel rods. "Rebars are the only reason some of those columns were left standing at all. This was an extremely powerful explosion. Material in the building was pulverized."
As far as the two, count 'em, two shock waves on the U of Oklahoma seismograph on April 19th? Mankin confirmed that.
"We had two events, ten seconds apart. The first one coincided in time with the explosion at the Federal Building."
"How far away is your station from the blast?"
"Twenty miles. Another seismograph, at the Omniplex, eight to nine miles away from the Federal Building, also recorded two waves."
"Is it possible that the falling of the building was the second signal, the second shock wave?"
"Of course we thought about that, but no, we've ruled that out."
"The US Geological Survey (USGS) has announced that they're satisfied there was only one shock wave. [And therefore only one bomb.] They seem to have a theory that would explain how two waves are one."
"Yes. They've made their announcement. As you probably have read, I felt their statement was premature, and since this is likely to come up at the trial, I thought they should have waited before deciding the issue. Their theory is, the same wave can travel at different speeds through different layers of rock [in the

earth]. So far we don't see how that would account for the ten-second separation between events on our seismograph."

Mankin made an interesting remark. "To get more on this, talk to our expert, Ray Brown."

I didn't tell him I had already spoken with Brown, who was obviously quite dissatisfied with the one-shock-wave theory.

I absolutely don't believe that Mankin and Brown could have been ignorant of the layers-of-rock phenomenon cited by the US Geological Survey, if it were a real or relevant factor. The USGS was, in effect, saying, "Look, we've JUST made a discovery. Bombs create a shock wave which travels along two different courses under the earth in two different layers of rock, and takes two different amounts of time to reach a destination 20 miles away. One route of travel is ten seconds slower than the other. Wow, we never knew this before."

Sure, and we'll give you a Nobel.

Continuing the Alice in Wonderland vibe, I call Channel 4 in OK City, an NBC affiliate. Because I've been told Brad Edwards, one of their reporters, is about to break a story on a Middle East connection to the bombing. Or he has already broken it.

On a Saturday morning (June 24), a reporter in the news room picks up the phone. I introduce myself and say, "I hear you guys have a story about a Middle East connection to McVeigh."

She says, "It's not a Middle East connection. It's a person who happens to be Middle Eastern."

"I understand," I say. "Have you broken the story yet?"

Pause. "We ran two different pieces. One about a week ago, and one a day ago."

"You did?"

Talk about containment. It's armed guards around the city and automatic censors on the phones and computers. Actually, a few guys in New York roll out of bed and take care of it. "No, Rex, we're not running the piece outside OK City. Say hi to Marge."

"Can I get tape?" I ask.

"No," she says. "We're under orders not to send out tape."

"Orders from who?"

"Our news director, Melissa Klinzing."

"Well, can you tell me what the two pieces you ran said? What was the gist?"

"We're not allowed to talk about it."

A news story is released on the air and no one can talk about it?

"What's the problem?"

"The news director can tell you. Talk to Melissa on Monday."

"Is she able to tell me what the stories said?"

"Yes. She can. But none of us. You know, she's afraid if anything untrue gets out, there's liability. She wants to be the one to deal with liability if that comes up."

Hand me my top hat, I'm going to the tea party.

(About two weeks later, I would be told that General Partin had been denied access to file footage at Channel 4. The footage was of the Fed Bldg. after the bombing. Somebody just wanted Partin to sit there at Channel 4 and look at tape. No go.)

AP releases a story about McVeigh, based on his first interview from jail, with Newsweek. McVeigh says he's going to plead innocent. The first he heard of the bombing was from the trooper who stopped him for no license plate on his car. He never said he was a prisoner of war, he claims. He was horrified that children were killed. After being arrested, he never limited his response to name, rank, and serial number. He didn't attend militia meetings.

On Monday Morning, June 26, I talk again to Ray Brown, the geophysicist at the U of Oklahoma at Norman. I'm trying to resolve a few things. If there were two events recorded at the U of Oklahoma seismograph on April 19th, two explosions, why were they so similar? Why did their signals look so much alike? (That is common knowledge now.) Was this because two bombs placed inside the building, identical devices, made those impressions twenty miles away at Norman?
If that was true, then what happened to the truck bomb? It didn't register at all at Norman? Is that possible?
"What you're suggesting could be true," Brown said, "except that there was the big crater in the ground under the truck. Something big caused that, and it would have sent a wave through the ground, and we would have picked it up on our equipment."

Brown then fed me a blockbuster: Even if only one signal had arrived at Norman from the Fed Bldg. on April 19, it could still "contain" two separate explosions, or more. The signal is a resolution, as it were, of a number of sub-signals.

JACKPOT. That opened the door wide to the possibility of a number of charges placed inside the Fed. Bldg.

Brown told me a couple of things I hadn't heard before.

"I talked to a lawyer," he said. "His secretary was inside the Federal Building. She was standing by a window. The window cracked, and then she got away from it and then she was blown across the room and landed in another woman's lap who was sitting at a desk. Another woman I know, Judy Morse, got under her desk after feeling the building shake, and before the glass flew."

This was inconsistent with the government scenario. The window glass should fly first. IF ONE BIG BANG OUT OF A TRUCK DID ALL THE DAMAGE TO THE BUILDING, forget the idea of a several-second delay between the first rumbling signs of trouble and the shattering of windows. Forget a single window cracking as a warning sign of disaster to come moments later. The sweep of the shock wave would have been immediate and total.

It wasn't.

I recounted some of my conversation about the pillars with General Partin.

Brown perked up and said very directly, "My first impression was, this was a demolition job. Somebody who went in with equipment tried to take down the building."

What stuck in my mind after the interview with Brown was, naturally, this: Nobody had admitted that one signal recorded on a seismograph could cover for several explosions at the Fed Bldg. That was key, and it made academic some of the fine points.

The July 3rd Newsweek interview of McVeigh was interesting.

McVeigh, a sergeant in the Army, won early promotion. His combat arms proficiency scores were in the top five percent. Newsweek gave these scores to a master sergeant currently in the Army. Not knowing whose records he was looking at, the soldier said, "He [McVeigh] would make a great infantry officer, tanker, artillery officer or combat engineer."

So the media-created stupid redneck is not so stupid. During the interview, McVeigh comes off as fairly bright.

What does this potential reshuffling of his portrait do to the government's OK City scenario?

Why is a smart soldier driving without a license tag after the blast? Why is he renting a Ryder truck and buying fertilizer that can be traced by a moron? Why is he driving away from the bombing with a Glock pistol and a knife on his person, and then showing them, volunteering them, to the trooper who stops him on the road?

Contradictions.

THE FOURTH IMAGE

This is some way to get news. To find out what Channel 4 in OK City said about the bombing, I have to call a friend down in the area and ask him what the hell he saw on the tube at 11pm. Who's kidding who?

Well, Channel 4 has indeed run two stories on an Iraqi soldier and McVeigh. From what I can gather it isn't just Middle East bashing. Channel 4 produced witnesses who said they saw McVeigh and the Iraqi soldier together in a bar, in OK City, the Saturday and Sunday before the bombing. The bombing took place on Wednesday, April 19th, so we're talking April 15th and 16th. The Iraqi soldier was driving a brown Chevy pickup. At least one of these witnesses talked to the Iraqi man in the bar and found out that he was, in fact, a former soldier in the Gulf.

Channel 4 has a separate witness who says she saw a Middle-Eastern-looking man speed away from the bombing in a brown pickup. Who says she told the FBI, who apparently haven't tapped him for questioning. This witness later identified the man she saw as the man in the bar with McVeigh. From photos.

Finally, the FBI itself, early on, announced they were looking for a brown pickup.

It's possible that this Iraqi soldier is one of several thousand who were relocated to the US by Clinton.

The term "Iraqi soldier" could suggest that Saddam of Iraq was trying to get revenge on the US. But the US government uses all sorts of strange cutouts in operations. These are people who have hard-to-trace connections with the CIA or Defense Intelligence, and so on.

The revelations from Channel 4 are very unusual and worth pursuing. People at the station have taken heat for trying to bring out this story, for actually tracking down and investigating leads, instead of passively accepting press releases from the government and running with them.

It's interesting to me that as I write this, as I check into the contradictions of the explosion, the New American Magazine of June 26 has come out with the best story on OK City so far. Interesting because the magazine is the reincarnation of older John Birch Society publications. Typically, mainstream reporters refuse to consider information from the left or the right, and consider themselves "objective centrists." Sure they are. What would your reaction be if a pawn in a chess game suddenly, on the board, rose up on his hind legs and said, "I'm an objective centrist."

The New American article, by Bill Jasper, centers around none other than General Ben Partin, he of the grid and columns, and his unsolicited report to the Congress on the April 19th disaster. It does the right things very straightforwardly. It brings out Partin's conclusions, recites his credentials, which are quite impressive, vis-a-vis weapons design and testing, far beyond what was mentioned in the CV forwarded to me. It asks other explosives experts to comment on Partin's conclusion that no ammonium nitrate bomb in a truck parked at the curb could cause the damage which the Fed Bldg. sustained. Just what you'd expect from an article and rarely find.

Jasper offers a Partin analogy that is telling. The

truck bomb that blew up the New York Trade Center, from the garage, created a "large cavity through several floors above and below the bomb," but, as Partin points out, "[a] column is still standing there in the middle of the cavity." [Time Magazine photo of March 8, 1993]

What does this suggest? That a whopper of a fertilizer device has serious problems taking out major columns and pillars, and that in the case of OK City, additional charges were needed AT THE COLUMNS to destroy those supports.

Five of the seven experts Jasper spoke with agreed with Partin's overall analysis. Sam Gronning, a licensed blaster in Casper, Wyoming, a man with 30 years experience, said, "No truck bomb of ANFO [ammonium nitrate slurry] out in the open is going to cause the kind of damage we had there [in Oklahoma City]."

Roger Raubach, a PhD in physical chemistry who once did research at Stanford, said, "General Partin's assessment is absolutely correct. I don't care if they pulled up a semi-trailer truck with 20 tons of ammonium nitrate; it wouldn't do the damage we saw there [in Oklahoma City]."

The two experts who disagreed with Partin cited the size of the fertilizer bomb at the Fed Bldg., and the similarity of the damage done to the Marine barracks in Lebanon, in 1983, with a truck bomb.

Partin responded to those criticisms by saying that, in Lebanon, "[T]he truck was driven directly under the building so that the explosion had maximum effectiveness against a much lower building with much smaller columns."

As far as the size of the OK City truck device is

concerned, Partin agreed that it was large, but he emphasized that people don't truly understand how fast the force of such an explosion, SET OFF IN THE OPEN, decays. Jasper states it clearly: "...if you put just a few feet of air between the explosive and a target, the blast wave drops from millions of pounds [of pressure] per square inch to thousands of pounds per square inch. It still makes an impressive boom, but has very little effect on heavy reinforced concrete."

Whereas if you place the right explosive charges directly on concrete columns, you overcome their upper limit of resistance, which is about 5,000 pounds of pressure per square inch.

That was what was necessary at the Fed Bldg.

Depending on how you look at it, the fact that major networks are not picking up on the evidence against a truck bomb is either a yawn, or staggering.

A story researcher for a local LA network, in a fit of loyalty to mainstream press, told me that networks often miss important stories because they, the stories, aren't easy to find, and "the networks wouldn't have heard about them."

I couldn't have said it better myself.

The networks hire people with tunnel vision, and then they send too many of them to absurd places to cover momentarily titillating events. On this basis, they pass by significant happenings on land, sea, and in the air. I personally can't raise myself to pity their incoherence. I believe, in fact, that I could run a small and tough local channel on a network affiliate's budget for makeup.

I finally spoke with Melissa Klinzing, the news director at Channel 4 in OK City. She says they don't send out tape on this Iraqi story because radio stations have been ripping them off, running the audio portion of their pieces on the McVeigh-Iraqi angle, and not paying the standard fee. WNBC-TV in New York is finally running a version of the story, but NBC itself, the network, won't take it, because Channel 4 in OK City won't tell them the names of the witnesses who saw McVeigh and the Iraqi soldier together. The witnesses are terrified and want anonymity. Therefore, NBC can't verify their bona fides.

There has to be more to this. When news reporters refer all outside queries on a story to the news director, which is what happened to me when I first called, you know there's some kind of pressure coming down on heads.

Klinzing confirmed that Channel 4 had three witnesses. Two of them spotted McVeigh and the Iraqi ex-soldier in a bar. The other witness saw the Iraqi man (whose name has not been released by Channel 4) speeding away from the bombing in a brown pickup.

Weeks ago, Channel 4 gave its information to the FBI, before it released the first piece. A detective that Channel 4 hired to watch the Iraqi spotted FBI watching him as well. But no word that the FBI has gone forward with this aspect of the case.

The Iraqi man states that he was handing out anti-Saddam pamphlets in Iraq. Channel 4 believes this is bogus. They believe he was a member of the Republican Guard in Iraq. Clinton brought over a number of defecting Republican Guard soldiers, and they have been resettled in the US. This man might be one of them.

The FBI won't confirm or deny anything.

Channel 4 didn't show the Iraqi's face on TV.

The Iraqi went to Channel 5 and 9 and told them he was innocent of any connection to the bombing. 5 and 9 ran a story putting down Channel 4's version of events. Channel 9 showed time-sheets which the Iraqi claimed proved he was at work, at his job in OK City, at the time of the bombing. Channel 4 then found several employees at that place of business who told them time sheets aren't used. They all punch clocks.

The Iraqi is now missing. No one seems to be able to find him.

Under PROFIT, the federal government has some, in case anybody doubts it. Profit from the building being blown up.

First of all, to anyone who has eyes, federal power is an army of locusts. Despite Republican downsizing talk, the overpowering trend involves more control of the citizenry, more Bill-of-Rights scrapping, more octopus-maneuvering, more taking over of local functions, more computerizing, more linkage. More corporate-government identity of interest and agenda.

An eradication of human civil rights is proceeding.

Before the April 19th bombing, two anti-terrorism bills were molding in Congress. Since the bombing, they have been scrapped, and new shiny versions, with the same repressive slants, have been pushed up before a Congress now rabid about taking out terrorists regardless of the facts, regardless of the cost to the Constitution.

The bills are S735, which, on June 7, passed the Senate, 91-8, and HR1710, which is ready to come out of Committee (as of June 29/95) and on to the floor, with an excellent chance of passing. Clinton will sign these bills into law.

They expand the government's wiretapping habit, allowing bugs on both phones and fax machines without a court order, if the Justice Dept. thinks a person may be conspiring to commit a terrorist act. These bills give the feds more access to private bank accounts, vehicle rental records, public storage facilities. They permit the Justice Department to bring in the military AS POLICE in certain specific situations-- thus breaking one of the fundamental legal walls between soldiers and law-enforcement officers in this country. They also allow the President, without proof, to call any foreign group represented with a chapter in the US a terrorist organization. Such labeling would keep a fingered group from legally raising funds.

And in these bills, the definition of a terrorist act changes a number of times. Which is, of course, crucial, because "terrorism" and "conspiracy to commit terrorism" become the triggers for putting the above-described invasions of privacy into effect. The loosest definition of a terrorist act offered is simply using a firearm to commit a crime.

The anti-terrorism bills make the offense of destroying or damaging government property, or any other property involved in interstate commerce, a federal offense, with a max of 25 years as the penalty. That's damage, as in breaking a door, depending on who is doing the interpreting.

This federalization of crimes formerly defined as state offenses continues, with support from both the left and the right. Federalization of crime, of course, means more computer links, pressure for national ID cards, more smart cards with bios and medical info and background imprinted, more nationalizing of all local police functions, more ATF and FBI on the scene, more private doors kicked in with defective or no warrants, more asset forfeitures, military called in to act as police, and, generally, longer sentences. In other words, more federal control over citizens.

Even HR 1488, a bill now under consideration to repeal the assault weapons ban, contains a provision which can make ALL crimes committed with a gun federal offenses.

HR 1544, still in Committee, redefines a paramilitary group as two or more people, with one as the "Commander," who have weapons and intend to commit any crime. Max penalty? Ten years, without an actual offense having been carried out. This is the so-called anti-militia bill.

In the climate created by the OK City bombing, all these bills, or the most sinister portions of them, have an excellent chance of passing. If they do, it will give the feds much more leverage over people. When Patriots say, "WE didn't kill those babies at Waco, WE didn't shoot Randy Weaver's wife in the face at Ruby Ridge," they are talking more than rhetoric.

And speaking of climate, try out FEAR. I have now, in the middle of July, interviewed a man who was near the bomb scene on the morning of April 19th. He has told me, off the record, very much off the record, that he heard at least two distinct explosions, possibly three. But definitely two. From his manner, and his background, I would say he is in his right mind, his memory is clear, and he is speaking the truth. He told me, briefly, with no desire to elaborate, that he did not want his name to be circulated.

I believe that, like any intelligent American, he recognized that after going on the record, he would be a person federal law enforcement agencies and intelligence people would want to interview. This prospect did not make him feel assured. It did not make him feel safe and warm. It made him feel wary. This is a common reaction. I have to join the millions of people who say, at one time or another, THEY'RE SUPPOSED TO WORK FOR US. This is not a trivial point.

Disclosure of facts pertaining to an ongoing crime investigation, of course, can be limited by police on the job, but this practice has become an Everest of secrecy in the world of federal investigation. It enables the fed cops and their bosses to claim primacy for their GENERAL interests over and above citizens'. Anytime, anywhere.

There is another witness to the blast. He has gone on the record. His name is Michael Hinton. He lived in the YMCA building in OK City in April. The morning of the explosion, Hinton came out of the Y and got on a bus, rode it a short distance, and changed buses. As he was getting on for the second time, he heard a blast and felt "a violent rumble under the bus...I heard two explosions, six to seven seconds apart."

"I assume you know that people are saying a second blast could actually be a reverberation, or the building itself falling down. And you feel you know the difference between that and an explosion?"

"Yes, I do," he said.

Hinton went to the public library and spoke with a friend, who also heard two, possibly three, explosions. Hinton has told his story to Channel 4 in OK City. It has not yet been aired.

There are witnesses who heard two blasts on April 19th, and those who heard one. That in itself, that difference, is more than just "you always get conflicting stories." The networks and major papers have taken the FBI's version, and the FBI wasn't there. That's called manufacturing reality.

"Well, yes, some people claim to have heard two explosions, but you know, in these cases you get echoes and bounces, and secondary waves. It's common."

"Sorry. Had to ask."

The march of the robots goes on.

Let me provide a bit of context for disaster scenarios, such as Oklahoma City.

At present, 300 transnational corporations own about 20% of the world's assets. This is like saying you own the United States west of the Mississippi and a lot of islands out in the Pacific.

These corporations have a problem. They are too effective. They can produce so much that, at full bore, they would end up selling their products too cheaply. If tomorrow fifty million new cars appear in showrooms around the world, the supply will so far exceed the demand that, by nightfall, Lexuses will be going for five thousand dollars. So these transnationals begin downsizing, to avoid full-bore production, and many,

many people are thrown out of work.

In addition, money markets, the trading of world currencies, are really a global gambling book that makes Las Vegas look like a crap game outside a candy store. A trillion dollars changes hands every day. 98% of that trading is pure speculation which has nothing to do with corporate production or investments in tangible assets. This gambling is carried on, for the most part, by speculators who couldn't care less about the future of nations, money-supplies, companies, other people.

That destabilizing money-trading situation, and the corporate overproduction problem, are crises looking for a disaster to happen. Such a disaster, involving bankruptcies, the collapse of markets like the NY Stock Exchange, would put huge numbers of people at risk and on the street.

Providing for this eventuality, elites naturally seek more control of the citizenry, so that, when things suddenly plummet, they can maintain civil order while they gobble up what suddenly has become a fiesta of bargains. Companies, banks, land, bonds, stocks, natural resources, governments, you name it. Everything goes up for grabs.

Anything that narrows freedom and the sense of freedom, now, works to keep people in line during such a huge down period. During the US depression of the 1930s, the political left in America became much stronger. The anti-corporate labor movement grew muscles. Between a thousand and fifteen hundred LOCAL CURRENCIES were issued by communities who rejected, in toto, the bankrupt Federal Reserve dollars. These events created anxiety for the wealthy one percent of the country. Things might have gotten out of hand. There was a danger of mass rebellion, decentralization, a power shift downward, and so on. World War Two not only solved a job crisis, it reunified the nation around an external threat. It temporarily eliminated the possibility of the disintegration of the body politic.

Now, in 1995, as the poverty figures continue to expand, the INDUCTION OF FEAR (e.g., OK City) and further erosions of the Bill of Rights help the top one percent keep people in line. The OJ trial, OK City, the NY Trade Center, the Menendez trial...these are Roman circuses that distract people during bad times. They also bring about more fear of violence, a tendency to lock doors, to stay inside. They divide people against each other, along racial lines, they increase suspicion. Divide and conquer certainly works to restrain citizens from joining together, from assessing their common economic problems, from recognizing their hypnotic trance--under which they imagine that the federal government, the issuer of paper money with eyeballs above triangles, is the source of wealth in the country. Because, the truth be told, no one in heaven or Earth has legislated that citizens must become poor because governments and their dollars become poor. The one group in America--regardless of what you think of it-- which comes the closest to understanding this is the Patriots. Patriots are willing, if necessary, to carry on their lives without bowing down to Federal Reserve dollars or federal persuasion. They are rebellious. They are interested in prosaic substances such as gold and silver, and I think they will, some of them, begin issuing their own currencies. They may be willing to organize in smaller communities and opt out of the system. Fifty or a hundred new communities pose no threat to big central power, but a quick five or ten thousand communities of various stripes and persuasions will set very loud bells ringing.

Therefore, for the elite of this country, who depend on a unity of currency, who depend on a wide acceptance of federal money and all that that implies, who depend most of all on a fear of federal power, the Patriots become a target. Oklahoma City provides the opportunity to focus that target.

"Let's make ALL the Patriots into dangerous nut cases. Not to be listened to. Not to be believed. Not to be trusted."

This is the operation currently underway, radiating out from Oklahoma City.

THE FIFTH IMAGE

Most Patriots believe the Federal Reserve System is a private corporation poaching off the federal government, disguising itself as part of the executive branch. Most Patriots believe that the Fed Reserve is actually a group of private banks who give permission for money to be printed in this country. The Constitution, of course, places the power to coin money in the hands of Congress. The framers of the Constitution were well aware that central banks could and would literally take over a country, through encouraging the accumulation of debt (to them) by its government...leading as certainly to rule by banks as the IMF (International Monetary Fund) leads to rule by banks in Third World countries.

Patriots believe that the Fed Reserve makes enormous profits from, in essence, running the money printing press in America. These profits are paid to the owners of the Fed Reserve banks in the form of interest on the face value of new money printed. Every time it's printed. About eight dollars and fifty cents interest for every hundred dollars newly introduced into the nation's money supply.

Most Patriots are against the personal income tax as a way of raising money to run the government.

Patriots believe that the Second Amendment allows for unrestricted gun ownership by citizens, which acts as a deterrent against unreasonable search and seizure by police. Jews for the Preservation of

Firearms Ownership--not specifically a Patriot group--has done considerable research to show that, prior to all major 20th century genocides, the governments which would go on to commit those genocides passed laws outlawing private gun ownership.
Most Patriots believe in a strict interpretation of the Constitution. They believe that powers not explicitly given to the federal government in its Articles are reserved for the individual states. Therefore they want a severe reduction of present federal powers.

I can't prove this, but I think that some Patriots, the ones who do serve racist agendas, want to use the shrinking back of the Constitution to achieve Neanderthal ends, such as the elimination of women's rights to vote and equality for all citizens. That's the kind of program that would be framed in the Stone Age by Stone Age people. But I know that other Patriots, including some who are now coming into the movement, have a completely different feeling and conviction about the meaning of their work. They see that many, many grassroots operations by citizens, many kinds of decentralization of power, are necessary if we are going to move into the 21st Century with any chance of offloading the top-down controllers of our society. And they do not favor restrictions of ANYONE'S Bill of Rights freedoms. (Estimates of the size of the amorphous movement called Patriot vary considerably...from two million down to four hundred thousand. Possibly seventy percent of the people who call themselves Patriots do not belong to militias.)

The federal government does not like to be the enemy of Patriots around the country. There is a chance that current skirmishes between certain Militias and the feds will erupt into violence.

On the other hand, the OK City incident--which increases the chance of that violence--appears to serve federal interests. Meaning what? Meaning that the current propaganda machine is discrediting Patriots right and left as nuts and building more confidence in Washington as the common person's best chance of security and safety.

Yet that propaganda program is also backfiring, because militia memberships are now on the rise. Interest in militias is building.

So OK City is doing two things at the same time. It is bringing more people into the Patriot movement, and it is accruing good will for the feds as the protectors of its citizens.

Overall, this is not a great formula for peace.

I would say, at this point, that if this Patriot-Washington conflict erupts into gunfire, it will be the feds that will orchestrate and expand it. And, contrary to some assessments, a serious attempt to wipe out the Militias would create, not set-piece, but guerilla warfare in parts of the US. Ongoing expanding guerilla warfare, in which Militia would be able to melt back into the general population at a moment's notice.

The feds obviously exist, in the long run, only through citizen good will and trust. The Patriots are relentless about exposing what they take to be our government's operations aimed at increasing control over the lives of people. The best and real Patriots are relentless about challenging both the left and the right, and this REALLY makes people nervous, because our government maintains itself through a front of left-right conflict. That is the choice we are given, that is the way the game is played. That is the horse race. You can have Bush or Clinton, Gingrich or Kennedy, Demo or Rep, capitalism or socialism...the one distraction that must be preserved is this war of ideas, of men, of campaigns, of laws, of caricatures, of media creations. Meanwhile, every reporter with a brain in this country knows that, in Washington, the politicos play to the crowd, just as they did in Rome. They affect sincerity, they support issues for emotional effect, they hide their hypocrisy, they pray for votes. Every news reporter with half a brain KNOWS THIS, and yet, to make a living, peddles the horse race, peddles the war between left and right and the hope of the next election, peddles the superficial differences between political creatures of the same stripe.

More and more Americans are waking up to this phony form of politics, and among them are people, of various voices, who say: "We can own guns, it's legal and guaranteed in the Constitution, and so we will. To protect ourselves against the possibility that the feds want to crush us and form a more fascist state."

Is that paranoia or common sense?

There is definitely merit in the idea that every adult citizen, if armed with a weapon he/she knows how to use, can stand as a bulwark against illegal search and seizure by the government.

How much good militias do, in the long run, as a defense against federal abuses depends on who these people really are, and what their agendas really are. It's not in the scope of this book to take on that issue full-bore, but it is clear that isolation of citizens from militias, the absence of dialogue, the absence of real exploration by citizens, and real understanding, is a major mistake. Just as it has been a real mistake for fifty years to avoid grasping the direction and personnel of our leadership in Washington. I'm NOT making an equivalence between the feds and the militias. I'm making an equivalence among all dumbed-out TV-ed out passive citizens.

And I'll say this: Although I don't agree with all the militia literature I read, part of this information has kept large numbers of people aware of fed government abuses against Americans. All in all, it's a hell of a lot more accurate than the CBS Evening News.

For those Americans who obviously disagree with the militias...I would like to see them build a better spaceship on their own. Build twelve.

THE SIXTH IMAGE

Finally, as of June 30, the Iraqi-McVeigh story is getting out through a few local TV stations. Seattle apparently has picked it up. New York has it. According to one report from a source in OK City, the FBI refused to question the Iraqi soldier spotted by witnesses in the bar with McVeigh. Why? Is the FBI trying to downplay this possible scenario? Is the limit of its serious inquiry "Patriots and people so connected?"

On February 9th of this year, Bill Clinton signed Executive Order 12949. It expanded the powers of a little-known federal court called FISA, named after the Foreign Intelligence Surveillance Act of 1978. This secret, yes, secret court, can give the green light to the Justice Dept. to carry out physical searches with no public warrant, without ever letting the target know he HAS been searched, and without ever presenting a list of items taken in the search.

According to Executive Order 12949, the person whose property is invaded does not have to be suspected of a crime. His belongings can be tossed because he is a member of a group, or has helped a group, which is labeled by the Dept. of Justice as being a threat to national security.

To top it off, any evidence obtained in this kind of

invasion can be used in a criminal trial, not merely for intelligence purposes. That is the new wrinkle.

Presumably, the sort of group a person would belong to that would trigger federal intrusion is a foreign organization. But in light of the OK City bombing, we can expect to see attempts to redefine national security. New groups, including Patriots, and those who help them, would be targeted. Especially since some Patriots, to distance themselves from the control of the federal government, technically reclassify themselves as resident aliens.

"Of course we can ransack your house. After all, you sent a fifty-dollar contribution to the Militia of Montana. You also received their analysis of corruption in the tax system."

"Sorry. Had to ask."

"Of course we can ransack your home. After all, you sent a hundred dollars to the Get the CIA Out of Guatemala Fund."

"Of course we can ransack your home. You sent twenty dollars to the Committee for the Study of Power in Transnational Corporations."

Executive Order 12949 rips a huge hole in the 4th Amendment to the Constitution--which, by the way, states:

"The right of the people to be secure in their persons, houses, papers, and effects against unreasonable searches and seizures, shall not be violated, and no Warrants shall issue, but upon probable cause, supported by oath or affirmation, and particularly describing the places to be searched, and the persons or things to be seized."

The practice which has been used to defend the Fourth Amendment is called the exclusionary rule. It throws out, from a trial, any evidence obtained in an illegal search.

However, since the beginning of Reagan's second term in office, a loophole has been used to travel through the exclusionary rule. Called "good faith," it asserts that evidence found during an illegal search, in which the justifying warrant was issued without probable cause, can still be used in a trial.

"We meant well."

Now, in pending House Resolution 666, and Senate Bill 3, we have an attempt to further enlarge the "good faith" concept. Evidence obtained in searches done without ANY warrant at all can be admitted in a trial. The Senate version makes citizen recourse after an illegal search, even if injury and property loss result, very difficult. This recourse would involve suing the federal government, and the limit on punitive damages is $10,000.

Truth be told, progressives who are repelled by the legislative assaults on the Fourth Amendment, mentioned above, have a great deal in common with many Patriots.

Thursday night, June 29th, there was a meeting in Oklahoma City. It was chaired by State Representative Charles Key. Families of people killed at the Federal Building attended. So did a few explosives experts, including General Partin. Most of the meeting was taken up with people asking about the federal money that was still owed to them in the form of relief, in the wake of the disaster. Toward the end of the meeting,

Representative Key made a rather astonishing remark. It was by way of confirming a charge leveled by a member of the audience. Without naming names, Key said two witnesses exist who, on the street after the April 19th explosion, were approached by two ATF employees. One of those employees said, in so many words, "Thank God we had a bomb scare yesterday. They told us we didn't have to come in today."

Key called for a state task force to do an independent investigation of the Federal Building tragedy.

In discussion from the audience, several people said they heard only one blast on the morning of April 19th, and several people said they heard two blasts. There is no indication that the FBI is giving this disparity any attention at all. The official scenario is in place, and it brooks no variations.

"Now all you people who heard two explosions...you're deluded or suffering from ear problems. You folks who heard only one blast are sane and good Americans."

This meeting is yet another example of news from within OK City that does not move to the country at large. It's called containment. You would think that the big daily papers and the TV networks had no reporters on the scene there at all. Here is a State Representative saying that the federal police are ignoring vital matters in their investigation...and it gets zero play.

"Well, he's just an Oklahoma guy, and all those cops in charge are from Washington."

Edye Smith may know something about ATF people not coming to work at the Federal Building on April 19th, the day of the bombing. Interviewed by Gary Tuchman of CNN, on May 23rd, just after the federal government formally imploded the remains of the Fed Bldg., she said, "We're being told to keep our mouths shut, not talk about it, don't ask questions...we just innocently ask questions, you know--where was the ATF? All 15 or 17 of their employees survived, and they live--they're on the ninth floor [of the Fed. Bldg.]. They were the target of this explosion and where were they? Did they have a warning sign? I mean, did they think it might be a bad day to go in the office? They had an option to not go to work that day, and my kids didn't get that option, nobody else in the building got that option...We just want to know, and they're telling us, `Keep your mouth shut, don't talk about it.'"

Two of Edye Smith's young children were killed in the explosion on April 19th.

Once you introduce the idea of foreknowledge of the bombing, some strange questions begin to accumulate. What kind of foreknowledge? Were ATF told they could stay out of work on the 19th because a) a bomb scare took place the day before, and b) people thought an incident would be tried, to mark the second anniversary of the Waco disaster? In that case, why weren't all employees who worked in or around the Fed Building "given that option?"

Oklahoma State Representative Charles Key has

told me that, on the morning of the bombing, at 7:15am, two witnesses saw local bomb squad people deployed at the front of the Courthouse near the Fed Bldg.

And one of the witnesses who says, on the record, that he heard two explosions shortly after nine in the morning on April 19th, has also said he witnessed what looked like a fire drill a week before. Michael Hinton, who lived at the Y, near the Fed Building, states that on the afternoon of April 12th, he saw about 300 people quickly move out of the Fed Bldg. and on to the street. Fire drill, bomb scare?

To top it all off, a respected reporter in OK City, who insists on staying off the record because he might otherwise lose his job, tells me the two witnesses on the street, just after the bombing, were told by ATF employees that ATF people didn't have to come to work that day because the bomb scare WAS THAT DAY, the 19th, the day OF the bombing, not the day before.

On Oct. 28th, 1993, the NY Times printed a piece by Ralph Blumenthal on the NY Trade Center bombing. The story involved an undercover FBI agent named Emad Salem, who had infiltrated the group planning to blow up the Trade Center. Salem was actually, according to his testimony, in a position to substitute harmless powder in the bomb, and this was in fact the FBI plan. When the bomb fizzled, they could move in and make arrests. In other words, they would have an attempted, rather than a planned crime to prosecute.

Salem secretly taped hundreds of hours of conversations he had with fellow FBI agents. These tapes, Blumenthal writes, "[portray] the authorities as in a far better position than previously known to foil the Feb.26 bombing of New York's tallest towers." Blumenthal also states that the plan to install the fake powder in the bomb "was called off by an FBI supervisor who had other ideas about how the informer...should be used, the informer [Salem] said."

In a taped conversation with FBI agent Nancy Floyd, Salem discusses an earlier talk he had with an FBI agent named John Anticev. Salem tells Floyd he had said to Anticev, "...now you saw this bomb went off and you both know that we could avoid that...Do you deny your supervisor is the main reason of bombing the World Trade Center?" Salem claims that Anticev did not deny it.

Captain Bill Citty of the Oklahoma City Police has called me and left a message on my machine. (His PR man Bill Martin has been out for two days, and isn't available to confirm he told reporter Phil O'Halloran mercury fulminate was found in the Fed Bldg.) The Captain himself relays that no one in the Police Department knows anything about finding the mercury. That includes Bill Martin. So by proxy, Martin has recanted his story.

THE SEVENTH IMAGE

Some people like to point out that McVeigh said he had a microchip implanted in him by the Army. "Obviously the kid is crazy. See?"
It turns out that the Department of Defense has been talking about this sort of thing for a long time. It's called identification technology, and it isn't hard to do. The Defense Dept. wants to track soldiers on the battlefield. A combination of chessboard fascination and finding lost men. And who knows what else.
In 1994, the FDA passed regulations governing the installation of microchips in artificial body parts. Each chip can contain the wearer's relevant medical info.
Transponders worn on collars are everyday items for pets. InfoPet, for example, is a well-known company that sells those products, which are read remotely by a scanner. Surgical implantation of the chip itself is a straightforward procedure.
Of course, if McVeigh is a dupe, a fall-guy being used by far more sinister types, then an implanted chip is a natural.
"We don't want to lose the kid. Where is he now?"
"Take it easy, chief. He just went into the fertilizer store. He'll be there for awhile."

OK City is going to be used to further gun-control in this country. I have read some very sensible information on gun control, and some very narrow information. Many people who normally say bright things about the ominous threats of big government, when faced with the gun issue, suddenly assume that federal police with guns is just a fine idea all the way down the line... we have to support them in their investigations of "the right people," and we need no protection from government force ourselves.

Sure.

Oklahoma State Representative Charles Key has been taking some hits from Oklahoma media. This is because he is seriously and publicly questioning the federal scenario on the bombing.

Key said to me on July 10, "I heard an audiotape of an individual who [while in the Federal Building combing through ruins] came across...a bazooka-like object. He didn't know what he had." The object turned out to be a tow missile.

What was it doing there?

I asked Key what is left on the Murrah site after the federal boys took down the rest of the building with a demolition.

"Nothing," he said. "They buried everything. There's just dirt."

"You mean they plowed everything under?"

"No, I mean they took it all out of there, transported it somewhere else and buried it. Now there's a fence around the site of the Federal Building, and no one can go in, unless you're accompanied by a federal policeman."

In other words, the remaining evidence about what kinds of bombs took out the Fed Bldg. is sealed up underground.
"Not only that," he said. "They can keep people from trying to dig up any fragments or rubble at the new site, by saying that, since human remains are probably in there too, it can't be opened."
"You mean, they'd cite bacterial contamination? Or disturbing the dead?"
"Disturbing the dead."

I was told that General Ben Partin had seen some new photos of the destroyed columns at the Federal Building. I called him. He told me they only confirmed what he thought already.
"[Explosive] charges were placed on columns."
"Where?" I asked.
"I would say on the third floor...it's simple. Those columns failed at the third-floor level."
Partin explained that he could see, from the texture of the columns at the places where they had been broken off, that the destruction was from a device, not from structural failure.
"The surface areas [of the columns] are smooth, the breaks are precise. If it were structural damage, we'd see rough surfaces and cracks. They aren't there."
I told Partin that containers of mercury fulminate had apparently been found in the Federal Building after the explosion. He said he'd heard the same thing: "[Reports] mentioned two or three five-gallon

containers. Mercury fulminate is normally a booster material. It's a high-energy explosive...if you placed a row of the containers against the columns [on the third floor], and wired them, it could take down the columns."

Sam Gronning, an explosives man from Wyoming with several decades of experience, said he knew General Partin "by reputation...I know he's got the background in explosions and investigation [of bomb damage]. As far as the explosion at the Federal Building is concerned, to get a perfect mix of a 4000-pound [ammonium nitrate] bomb, the oil and the fertilizer, you'd have to spend days stirring. If it's not mixed properly it won't go off. And then you have to use it pretty quick or the oil will settle and it won't go off.

"Look at the [Federal Building]. It looks like a demolition."

Roger Raubach, a PhD in physical chemistry, former Stanford researcher, a man with a wide-ranging background in both physical and analytical chemistry, echoes Partin.

"The effect of explosives lessens dramatically with distance. You have a spherical expanding shock wave...it doesn't take long for the damage to drop off. How far was the truck bomb from the Federal Building, twenty or thirty feet? You have to knock out a whole wall of building first. A planar surface like that absorbs energy from the blast and diminishes it.

"Ammonium nitrate is not a very efficient explosive,

unless you compact it into a hole in the ground. It's been used that way for seventy or eighty years, as a mining explosive. It doesn't pulverize things. It loosens up the dirt. In mining operations, they don't want things reduced to dust."

That was very important. I told Raubach that Charles Mankin, of the Oklahoma U Geological Survey, saw a lot of pulverization in the wreckage of the Fed Bldg.

"High-velocity devices [set off] inside the building could cause that."

Then Raubach said, "I'm not a wild-eye right-wing radical. I'm a scientist. I'm just telling you what was observed. All the AP UPI type-stuff, what is bandied about by Dan Rather...all that is b.s. This is the textbook explanation I'm giving you."

THE EIGHTH IMAGE

A reporter named Jerry Bohnen, who is the news director at K-TOK radio in Oklahoma City, was approached by a homeless man who said he'd been drinking with McVeigh on April 18th, the day before the bombing.

The homeless man said he was hanging around near an OK City McDonald's at Sheriden and Western, when McVeigh drove by in a brown pickup and yelled, "Hey, want to have a few beers?"

The homeless man said yes, went across the street and bought two quarts at the Total Store.

There is some question about whether this was in the morning, or at night about 9.

To check this story out, Bohnen goes into the Total Store and speaks with an employee, Ron Williams, who confirms that, on April 18th, a homeless man of the right description came in and bought two quarts of beer.

The day after Bohnen's visit, FBI people showed up at Total and took away tape from the surveillance cameras.

I spoke with Ron Williams. He said the homeless man came into his store about 9 at night on the 18th. Also, there was a Ryder truck parked at the McDonald's at the time.

David Hall, who has made documentaries on Waco and the Weaver tragedy at Ruby Ridge, told me that he has spoken with the Nichols brothers. Terry says that McVeigh was at the McDonald's on the night of the 18th. Purpose? A meeting.

Hall states that Terry told him McVeigh was there to meet with money men. For a payoff, which did occur. The sum was apparently two thousand dollars.

Another OK City reporter I've mentioned before--who will not go on the record for fear of losing his job--has a local Middle-Eastern source who also claims this payoff-meeting took place on the 18th.

According to Bohnen, the FBI have questioned the homeless man on at least one occasion, on or about April 27 (not necessarily about a payoff). A few days after that, agents were seen in a run-down section of OK City looking for him again.

It is possible McVeigh was paid for simply showing up in the Ryder truck with some bags of fertilizer inside.

"Okay, Tim, now get lost for a few hours. We'll meet you by the bridge at 7am. You'll get another two grand then. You'll park the truck in front of the Fed Bldg., like we said, at a few minutes before nine, and you'll walk away. No problem."

"What kind of bomb is this again?"

"We told you. A small boom. We're setting off little bombs in a few places to commemorate Waco. And the American War of Revolution. The two-hundredth anniversary is tomorrow. Let's not forget that. Nobody'll get hurt. Just bangers."

THE NINTH IMAGE

The law enforcement people at the Federal Building have covered up facts of the explosion. Their interpretation won't stand up. The single truck bomb is a hoax. At some level of command and control, this had to be an intentional diversion away from the truth.
What was the purpose of that lying, that cover-up? To keep people from knowing that some faction, some intelligence/military group blew up the building? To keep people from inferring that McVeigh was being operated by a handler, was being guided into his actions?
Why say that an intelligence/military group did the real killing at the Fed Bldg.? Because these are the people who know how to pull off such an operation, unless you want to look around for a commercial demolition firm or a bunch of chemistry teaching assistants from a college.
Of course, rogue military types, formerly associated with government work, have been in the free-lance business for some years now, as we saw in Iran-Contra, so that is a possibility too.
We know that the payoff for murder in OK City is repressive legislation and a discrediting of Patriot groups. We know that both these outcomes fit with the underlying machine-language of the federal-government agenda--which adds up to power cynically wrapped in the American flag, and control over citizens' lives.

It is likely that, even if foreign pros did this job for their own reasons, once the investigation got underway, it was determined that McVeigh would become the symbol for "all those Patriots." The investigation would move only toward a conclusion of Patriot guilt, and away from any foreign connection.

"Yeah, we hit the Middle-East image pretty good on the Trade Center thing. We don't need to go back over that territory again, at least for right now. Let's trample on the Patriots, the freedom and independence baloney."

"Good thought. Independence equals mass murder. That'll play. If your thoughts and feelings carry you out beyond the scope of government as the boss, you're dangerous, you'll probably turn violent, and you'll have to be hamstrung and executed. I like it."

There is another level to this. You can see it in the pattern of destruction at Waco. Objects in the landscape around the Koresh compound crushed for no apparent reason. A water tower, a bus, go-carts.

The desire for violence.

The name of the government operation at Waco was Showtime.

In addition, a new funding period was approaching for ATF. They were looking for Congressional dollars, tax dollars, to buy more expensive toys. They wanted to be on a par with their "better cousins," the FBI.

Waco would be their gratifying graduation into the mainstream of America, their moment for big-time

press coverage.
All of the above would be signs of law-enforcement out of control.
And there is always pressure to put on a first-rate attack. A bad performance equals personal humiliation.
"Winning is everything."
"We wasted those suckers."
Suppose those suckers are innocent American citizens?
Who's fighting who?
Law enforcement out of control, playing the wrong game, acting out the discipline of the attack dog, who has been trained to hate, to go after whoever his master commands, who has a pent-up need to do violence.
The flip side of this is, never admit your group, your master made a serious mistake. Never admit that your operation was a disaster, that innocent people and the Constitution were trampled underfoot. The Constitution is an annoying piece of history for these people, nothing more, a document which is given its due in certain administrative settings where reassurance and PR are required.
THIS is the behavior of a cult.

On May 15th, 1995, the National Rifle Association printed an extraordinary full-page ad in newspapers around the country. The ad mentioned that both the American Civil Liberties Union and NRA, as well as other organizations, had petitioned President Clinton to launch a full-scale investigation of abuses against citizens by federal law enforcement agencies.

It's worth noting that a group of black ATF agents has filed a suit against the ATF for widespread discrimination. Among the charges mentioned, one involves white agents in Oklahoma City, in 1991, decorating their walls with a `State of Oklahoma Nigger-Hunting License,' and a Ku Klux Klan business card.

The last time the ATF was investigated by Congress, in a Senate Subcommittee on Treasury hearing in 1980, the overall conclusion was: "...it is apparent that enforcement tactics made possible by current federal firearms laws are constitutionally, legally, and practically reprehensible.

"...These practices, amply documented...leave little doubt that that the Bureau has disregarded rights guaranteed by the Constitution and laws of the United States...It has trampled upon the Second Amendment by chilling exercise of the right to keep and bear arms by law-abiding citizens...It has offended the Fourth Amendment by unreasonably searching and seizing private property...It has ignored the Fifth Amendment by taking private property without just compensation and by entrapping honest citizens without regard for their right to due process of law...The rebuttal presented to the Subcommittee by the Bureau was utterly unconvincing...Evidence was submitted establishing that approximately 75 percent of BATF gun prosecutions were aimed at ordinary citizens who had neither criminal intent nor knowledge..." Read that last sentence again.

When a law enforcement agency can't find real crimes to prosecute, and yet must show "results" to justify their existence and their annual bloated budget, it stands to reason that, like any bureaucracy, they will invent crimes to pursue. They will slant evidence, ignore evidence, they will do whatever is necessary to make themselves look good. I've used the ATF as an example here. But I believe that all fed enforcement and intelligence agencies are operating far, far beyond any safe concept of Constitutional restraint.

Disasters can be staged in two ways. Before, and after. People can blow up a building and kill citizens, or they can simply take over an already blown-up building and sculpt imagery to serve their purposes.

The truck bomb did not leave unexploded ANFO all over the city. ANFO is ammonium nitrate plus fuel oil. You would expect this kind of residue from the truck explosion. It's normal. You would also expect black soot in a fairly wide area. That did not occur either. That tells you the following: The ammonium nitrate inside the Ryder truck was exploded by a very precise method.

This high-level explosion would still not account for the pattern of column damage in the Fed Bldg., particularly the anomalous destruction of column B3 and the survival of adjacent B4 and B5--but the bomb would have been built by pros. Talking timing and coordination of detonation among the various plastic containers in terms of milliseconds.

So, from all sides, we get the interpretation: outside professional help.

McVeigh himself, in the Army, attended three schools: Primary Leadership Development, Fort Riley; Infantry, Fort Benning; and Bradley Fighting Vehicle Transition, Fort Riley. In this training, he would not have been taught how to produce no-residue high-end ammonium nitrate explosions.

In building a case against McVeigh, the prosecution and the FBI will bring forward their parade of witnesses. So far, the only one widely known is Michael Fortier, an Army buddy of McVeigh who, in February, 1994, got him a job at Tru Value in Kingman, Arizona. It is instructive to see Fortier's reversal. Within ten days of the bombing, he told reporters, "I know my friend. Tim McVeigh is not the face of terror as reported on Time Magazine. Everyone just assumes he did it, automatically... The only fact is that the man was caught speeding on a highway in Oklahoma...In America, we believe people are innocent until proven guilty."

Now Fortier, who apparently faces a separate weapons charge, has said he and McVeigh went to Oklahoma City before the bombing and looked over the Federal Building.

What made him change his mind? A deal to escape prosecution on the guns charge?

Makes you wish there were a law requiring all

conversations between defendants and police to be taped and played, in toto, on cable. C-SPAN 4.

What other witnesses will the FBI bring up to the stand? The three unnamed people who were at the Federal Building on the morning of April 19th, before the bombing. They have IDed McVeigh from an FBI artist's sketch. They say McVeigh was hanging around the building before 9am.

Then there is the unnamed friend who saw the artist's sketch on TV and called the FBI and said McVeigh had been in the Army, was a right-wing nut, and had visited Waco because he was so upset about what federal police had done there.

There was another unnamed person who saw McVeigh drive away from the Federal Building just after the bombing.

The FBI also has an OK City meter maid who will say she saw McVeigh, early on the morning of the 19th, driving a Ryder truck toward the front entrance of the Federal Building.

Shortly after this, a woman driving on NW 5th had to brake hard to avoid hitting McVeigh, she says, as he slowly walked away from the Fed Bldg. This is still before the bombing.

Apparently a man coming out of the Journal Record Building, near the Fed Bldg., saw McVeigh and another man driving at a fast clip away from the Fed Bldg. This seems to be before the bombs went off--in which case, it might contradict the witness above who apparently saw McVeigh drive away just AFTER the bombing.

Who are all these witnesses, particularly the three who IDed McVeigh originally, from the sketch, as hanging around the Fed Bldg. just before the bombing, and the friend who saw the sketch on TV and called the FBI?

Will Mr. Jones, McVeigh's lawyer, have the time or inclination to examine their backgrounds with a fine tooth comb? Will he be able to discover any existing "conflicts of interest?" Will he press this sort of investigation, or will he back off and ignore it?

What exactly did FBI officers say to these witnesses?

Of course, all this crosses over into the area of prepping witnesses for trial, rehearsing them, honing their stories. But, as with Robert Shapiro and the OJ defense team's extraordinary challenge of DNA procedures, in a trial of this magnitude Lawyer Jones could challenge prepping to the hilt. As in exerting undue pressure. Since the official analysis of the explosions themselves has been lies built on lies, it ought to tip him off that illegal behavior is the order of the day.

However, I think this lawyer will not walk the whole distance.

Her blonde hair is arranged, some would say, artfully. But it's obvious that the spray is shellacking it, and the pile of the layers is following a simpleton's idea of impressive architectural elevation. Her hair is an upstairs-downstairs condo that people with no taste pay for through the nose.

She is winding up her evening segment on OK City. The bombing. She can read copy. A light blue shadow of intelligence hovers around her eyes.

She can affect having had a college education. The audience buys it.

She is called a reporter. She follows the credo that once official agencies set the tone of a story, divergent scenarios are "weird." She can show a bit of sympathy for the persons who back the unofficial, and therefore, wrong horse. She can.

But her subliminal power rests on the American premise that to promote unusual realities is to reject BEAUTY. BEAUTY IS SHE, SHE IS BEAUTIFUL. SHE HAS THE OFFICIAL WORD. THEREFORE IT HAS TO BE ACCEPTED. BECAUSE TO ACCEPT IT IS TO ACCEPT HER, THE BEAUTIFUL. WHAT FOOL WOULD REJECT HER?

To wind up her segment, she dutifully mentions that some people think the government itself blew up the Federal Building in Oklahoma City. But no proof has been offered.

Ah.

Well that's it then.

THE TENTH IMAGE

A conspiracy is malice aforethought. A community of interest is vultures with different agendas feeding off a good thing. As cruel as it may sound, Oklahoma City is a good thing for many people: The federal government is suddenly seen as useful by citizens, the FBI and ATF are on the case, they have visibility, they can now say with assurance that they need larger budgets...after all, crime, as evidenced by the tragedy at the Fed Bldg., is expanding. Who will stop it?

Truth be told, we are in an epidemic of the manufacture of crime. On top of actual crime.

Increased penalties for drug use, and the so-called war on drugs, go nowhere in stemming the flow of illegal substances into American communities, but they surely provide law enforcement people with more to do. There are always sting operations to mount; homes to break into; piddling quantities of contraband to seize; houses and cars and boats and cash to steal from citizens (called asset forfeiture) and divide up among avaricious law enforcement officers.

Since the middle of Ronald Reagan's sojourn in the White House, we have had a new asset forfeiture law, under which police can PERSONALLY KEEP the bounty they take as forfeit from SUSPECTED criminals.

"You are planning to sell six pounds of pot, and you are going to sell it out of your condo, so we're taking the condo. We're not booking you yet, but we might (if we can find any real evidence). In the meantime, the only way you can get your house back is by proving you are innocent of any intent to commit a crime. Just try."

"Okay, guys, guess we're the proud owners of this new condo. Party on. We can keep it for ourselves, or we can sell it and divide up the proceeds. What do you think? Take a vote? Could be a nice place for weekends. Barbecue on the balcony, pool and tennis courts. You know, we could probably entrap a dozen other people in this development...a dozen? Hell, if we start having knocked-out parties, we can probably tangle up half the residents on the block. Push a little coke, acid, pot, take names and snapshots. End up owning the whole development through forfeits. Go into the real estate business."

Why is the ATF, as of 1980, making 75% bogus arrests? Because they have to invent it. They can't find enough people who illegally possess weapons to fill up an eight-hour day.

As the newspapers and TV push crime as the major item of their commerce, it appears the country is made up of nothing but lunatic murderers. Of course, when your TV station has the AP to rely on, and that organization is scooping up crime stories from Maine to Florida in its net, twenty-four hours a day, you can lead off a broadcast in SEATTLE with a murder of a child in a rowboat in DELAWARE and paralyze your viewers for sixty seconds. With two hundred fifty million people and fifty states to draw upon, you'll never run out of grisly quick-hitters.

Fed law enforcement is thus sold twice a day, on the tube, every day.

If the truck bomb was wired by a pro, in order to produce a "clean explosion," there is a chance McVeigh never saw how things were rigged in the back of the Ryder.

"Don't go back there. You might mess up the cord."

McVeigh might have thought the blast would be smaller. Much smaller. In which case, he was quite a dupe.

He's driving away down the highway at ten in the morning thinking the Ryder truck set off " a symbolic explosion," to "show those feds we mean business."

In the current atmosphere, fueled by the greed of officers of the law who want to seize more and more American property and make it their own, one should never dismiss the possibility that a disaster like OK City was spotted, in its early stages, by federal police agencies, and allowed to progress along its rails.

Because fame, prestige, bigger budgets, and more power would lie in store for the officers and the agency who could make a bust of such magnitude IN THE NICK OF TIME. That NICK would be necessary to provide the punch, the drama, the sense of urgency. The adrenaline kick that would put things over the top, that would galvanize the media and public.

Who cares about wimpy arrests made only two weeks after the plot is hatched?

Larry Potts, in charge of the FBI investigation in OK City, has been taken off the case and demoted down to invisibility. Only ceaseless campaigning by Patriots about Pott's role at Ruby Ridge and Waco has made this possible.

On the morning of April 19th, 1775, a British major named John Pitcairn mounted a search, with six light infantry companies, for American patriot weapons depots. On Lexington green, he encountered seventy local villagers. They were armed. They were not eager for a fight, because British numbers were much too great. On the other hand, they refused an order from Pitcairn to lay down their weapons.
A shot was fired.
This was the beginning of the American War of Revolution.
On the same day, a similar event occurred at Concord. A British attempt at gun control failed in a large way.
On April 19th, 1993, at Waco, Texas, US federal police staged their final raid on David Koresh's church, a place where, supposedly, too many weapons were stored. After announcing on loudspeakers that they were not attacking, these federal officers carried out a two-tank assault on the back of the Koresh building, out of view of TV cameras. FBI slides obtained much later, during legal discovery, clearly show that,

contrary to the presumed aim of opening up holes for Branch Davidian members who wanted to escape, the tanks rammed the back of the building over and over again, to crush it, to erect an impenetrable barrier of plaster, metal and glass, to cave in the roof of the building. The net effect of this attack was to seal in Branch Davidian members so that, when the fire started--at the back, not the front of the building-- escape from the flames would be extremely difficult. In addition, the Davidian compound had been surrounded with razor wire, another barrier against exit.

Since the FBI had cut off all electricity in Koresh's building, the church members were using fuel lanterns. It's easy to imagine that, under the intense pounding of the government tanks at the back of the building, the fire began. The FBI was certainly able to foresee this eventuality, particularly since, that day, 25-mile-an-hour winds were whistling around Waco...and moving through the punched holes in the Davidian building.

Eighty-six people died.

April 19th, 1775. April 19th, 1993.

Is it merely a coincidence that that date, called Patriot's Day, and well-known to Patriots, was chosen for the final destruction of Koresh's church?

As an act of provocation, the date would be perfect for creating further conflict between Patriots and the federal government.

The demonizing of targets is a familiar ploy. Sometimes this is called blame the victim. African

Americans, Latinos, Asians, Indians have been, of course, subject to it for a very long time. The government can attack people with virtual impunity when they are sufficiently demonized. And there exist numbers of PR-spinners who will dream up new ways to achieve this form of propaganda.

Now we have the demonization of people the government has attacked at Waco--and the current agitprop blitz against Patriots. Listening to nothing but media spin on these people, one would be prone to say, Let the government punish them as they will, they are very bad.

In other words, suspend the laws of the land, forget due process, ignore judicial restraint, and just ASSAULT.

This is the power of media invention.

Suppose Patriots and Indians, African Americans, Latinos, and Asians of this country begin to build common ground. Could it happen?

It is important to realize that American media immediately jumped on McVeigh as a crazy who was out of control, although, in fact, they had no reason to assume this. They were taking cues, they were behaving like the obedient boys and girls they are. They were demonizing McVeigh from the first moment, and practicing a time-honored and useful form of mind-control on the American public.

THE ELEVENTH IMAGE

The explosion again.
Looking over General Partin's letter to Congress, other specific points he makes are worth mentioning. I'll lay out the rows of columns. Row A is the north side of the building, which is the front.

C1 C2 C3 C4 C5 C6 C7 C8 C9 C10 C11
B1 B2 B3 B4 B5 B6 B7 B8 B9 B10 B11
A1 A2 A3 A4 A5 A6 A7 A8 A9 A10 A11

Column A7 is a monster pillar. Partin remarks, "If column A7 was brought down by the truck bomb [impossible], then most of the much smaller columns B1, B2, B4, B5 and B6 should not be still standing but they are."

Partin continues, "Conversely, a truck bomb that could not bring down columns B1, B2, B4 and B5 could certainly not be expected to collapse...a much heavier column A7. Thus columns A7 and A8 should still be standing which they are not."

And then Partin comments on the destruction of column A7: "For a simplistic blast truck bomb, of the size and composition reported, to be able to reach out on the order of sixty feet and collapse a reinforced column base the size of column A7 is beyond credulity. Even bringing down B3 [which did go down] at its range is highly suspect. Glass and plastic

can be broken a long way off with explosives but not heavy, reinforced, concrete columns."
 The truck was parked approximately between columns A4 and A5 and about twenty feet down (north) from them.

Reviewing what an off-the-record explosives expert told me over a month ago, I see that his objection to the truck-bomb theory becomes a lot stronger. He said he would have expected a truck bomb that caused the damage it (supposedly) did to go all the way through the back wall of the building. It didn't. Rearranging his statement a bit, the observation is devastating: If the truck bomb really took out all those big columns, it would have gone through the back (south) wall of the building like a knife through butter...BUT THAT DIDN'T HAPPEN.
 This is all a hoax.

The pattern of destruction emanating from a truck bomb blast would be circular as it moves out. But nearly all of the damage was to row A. Columns A2 through A8 went down. This does not make sense. Circular shock waves don't create linear left to right patterns of destruction.
 Another way of making General Partin's point.

THE TWELFTH IMAGE

The ANFO explosion of the truck bomb was clean. It left no soot. And according to one observer, only a minor amount of unexploded fertilizer was found on the scene, near the crater where the truck had been. Pros built that bomb. It takes a pro to leave almost no fertilizer and no soot.

A real pro, however, would know that this truck bomb wouldn't take out the building's columns.

In that case, why bother to fiddle with ANFO and put together a rather delicate device in the back of the truck? A device that might not detonate all the way.

There was one reason. In order to implicate McVeigh, whose fingerprint, the FBI claims, is on the receipt for a few thousand pounds of fertilizer.

A real pro would build himself a small ANFO bomb that would leave a bit of fertilizer around for the cursory investigators. That would link the amateur (McVeigh) to the job. But the pro, going for the sure thing, would put something straightforward, reliable, fairly powerful and very loud inside the truck, to make sure it provided cover, an adequate diversion from the main event--which of course was the string of charges placed inside the building.

McVeigh, acting under orders, buys a large amount of fertilizer. McVeigh is told this fertilizer will be used in several explosions, in different locales, all perhaps to be set off on the morning of the 19th of April, to mark the anniversary of Waco and the 1775 start of the American Revolution. The truck bomb outside the Fed Bldg. will be a minor affair. Just a firecracker.

In that case, McVeigh never saw what was really in the back of the truck.

It also makes more sense of the weird fact that McVeigh lets the arresting Oklahoma Trooper know he has a gun under his windbreaker. McVeigh doesn't think he did anything serious. He doesn't understand his true situation. He doesn't want to kill the cop. He has no intention of doing so.

THE THIRTEENTH IMAGE

Who would have access to the Fed Bldg.? Who could place charges at the columns along the third floor? First of all, the time involved would be relatively brief. The separate charges would not have to be connected by any physical cord. They could have air-pressure detonators. That means that when the truck bomb produces a sudden change in pressure, the interior charges on the columns automatically explode, all at the same time.

Some columns in the Fed Bldg. were visible as interior decoration, and some required access through maintenance ports.

The third floor was taken up mainly by credit union offices. There was also an Army recruiting office. Men disguised in military uniforms would have no problem moving around on that floor. The charges themselves could be placed as quickly as one would hang paintings.

Gaining entrance through the maintenance ports would present no insuperable difficulties, either.

Inserting explosives in visible columns so that they wouldn't be noticed would require evening access, for drilling holes, refinishing, and so on. Overall, it appears that the evening before the bombing would be the time for installing all the charges.

It could be revealing to reconstruct which columns (that were taken out) were visible inside the building, and which required access through maintenance ports. Perhaps there is a pattern.

Various kinds of pros could have carried out this operation.

The main jumping off point is this: Who is covering up the true details of the explosion?

American law enforcement people. FBI. Until a few days ago, Larry Potts was their leader on the scene. Potts who, by many accounts, contributed heavily to the tragedies at Ruby Ridge and Waco. But he was really only a minor bureaucrat.

Shall we apply the old maxim, The cover-up leads to the conspiracy?

Whoever has limited the parameters of the investigation for the FBI is clearly covering up the truth about the bombs used and where they were located.

That person(s) stands a very good chance of being on the command line--in other words, inside the federal government, since the FBI is being controlled by him, and to an absolutely perfect degree. So far.

I assume that this controller is outside the FBI, since decisions of this magnitude would have to come from someone more powerful than the Bureau director.

If what we are hearing about McVeigh's point of view is correct, he would only have allowed himself to be recruited by people he assumed were Patriots.

There was a good reason never to show McVeigh

what was in the back of the Ryder truck: to conceal the presence of a non-ANFO bomb there. A non-ANFO bomb would instantly reveal that he, McVeigh, was ignorant of the real operation, that he was probably a dupe. No one wanted McVeigh to see a device whose power was greater than he expected, either.

"Hey, what the hell is this? I thought you said it was only a big firecracker? Count me out!...Who the hell are you, anyway?"

I believe it is probable McVeigh was recruited only to help set off a small device...as a symbolic gesture. Why bother waiting around to find a volunteer who would overtly agree to kill and injure hundreds of innocent Americans, including children? It's much easier to find an ex-soldier who wants a little action, who's angry at the government, who wants to make a statement, who wants to feel powerful for a day.

The classic fall-guy operation.

Whoever recruits McVeigh pretends to be a Patriot, and he looks American, not Iraqi. If there is an Iraqi connection, it could be that the American source of the operation is using an Iraqi cutout, a man who will oversee a part of the action. Who, in fact, can be spotted speeding away from the bombing; who, if necessary, can be busted and not be able to point a finger at any American group.

At some point in the command structure of the operation, McVeigh's fake-Patriot recruiter and the person(s) who narrows the scope of the FBI bombing-investigation overlap. Probably not knowingly, but through their mutual connections, they overlap.

A fake-Patriot recruiter who is American. A person within the federal government who can tell the FBI to limit their investigation. To me this sounds like a home-grown intelligence/military operation.

Purpose? As I outlined: to bring about more repressive legislation, to narrow freedom, to demoralize Americans, to induce fear, to discredit the Patriots, who--regardless of how you may look at them--are the most powerful force in America for rampant decentralization of federal power.

If, however, an outside pro team from a foreign country did the bombing, conceived it and did it, then the person(s) currently distorting the FBI investigation of the explosion is using a fortuitous opportunity to discredit the Patriots. In that event, he would have stepped up to become one of the chief conspirators, and would have involved the federal government, since he is obviously an employee of that government.

At this time--and reporters in OK City are moving ahead full steam on it--a Middle-East connection to McVeigh and Terry Nichols is being researched. The Iraqi who was IDed speeding away from the bombing in a brown pickup, the man who was featured by Channel 4 in two stories, the man who is now missing, was apparently acquainted with a certain Middle-Eastern businessman in OK City. That businessman, according to one reliable reporter on the scene, was a regular visitor to Las Vegas. On at least one occasion, McVeigh and this man were staying at adjoining hotels in Vegas. The apparent reluctance of the FBI to press ahead on this aspect of the investigation may be the result of an order from above to sidestep it. Why? Because, if an Iraqi ex-Republican Guard soldier has any connection to the tragedy at the Federal Building, and he is one of those soldiers the White House is responsible for resettling in the US, Mr. Clinton's political career is over.

The conclusions that fit the facts best are these: McVeigh was not aware he was recruited as part of a devastating plot to destroy many lives at the Federal Building on April 19. He thought he was doing something wild and outlandish that would not cause deaths. He may, in fact, have been paid to deliver the Ryder truck into OK City the night before the bombing. He is a delivery man. He never sees what is in the back of the truck, and has no idea that devices have been placed on pillars in the Fed Bldg.

When State Trooper Hangar stops McVeigh for driving with no license plate, McVeigh does not know what happened at the Murrrah Building. He shows his gun and knife to Officer Hangar, thinking that at most he's going to face a concealed weapons rap. He tells the cop he has a gun under his jacket so the cop won't get nervous and shoot him when he sees the Glock.

"What's that bulge under your windbreaker, son?"
"Officer, I have a weapon. I want you to know. I'm

not going for it. It's a gun."
"Slowly unzip the jacket..."
"Yessir."

A person(s) highly placed in the federal government controls and narrows the FBI investigation of the bombing. This accounts for the apparent massive stupidity on the part of the Bureau in ignoring how the building was actually taken down. The investigation is steered to blame the whole plot on McVeigh and Terry Nichols. And, therefore, to discredit, by association, all Patriots as violent nutcases.

Are there any FBI agents left with high-enough ideals to come forward and state, for the record, that their investigation is being managed, that they are essentially being ordered to lie to the American people and the families of those who died in the April 19th explosion?

The machine developed in the media to discredit the Patriots stems from their danger to Washington. They are bringing in new adherents every day. Many of these people no longer fit the old profile of ex-Army guys with guns. Many are interested in legally, and peacefully, withdrawing from the entire federal system of control in America. Increasingly sophisticated blueprints for doing just this are being developed by Patriot researchers. The movement is called Sovereign Citizenship. It entails the use of legal strategies to opt out of paying federal taxes, opt out of the Social Security apparatus (or any system of national ID), opt out of the need to carry licenses, such as driver's licenses. Opt out of the need to obey certain kinds of summons. Opt out of any inferior status vis-a-vis the federal government. The blueprints for pulling all this off are different from older versions used by, say, tax resisters in the 1960s. These new formal plans are based on disentangling a whole series of definitions of the United States as an entity, definitions which seem, on certain levels, to have established the federal government as a corporation rather than a nation.

Contrary to what certain angry pundits believe-- pundits who feel they are being intellectually outflanked by self-educated dyed-in-the-wool Patriots-- these systems of withdrawing from mainstream citizenship, and raising up a whole OTHER category called Sovereign Citizenship, could cause the federal government considerable headaches. These Patriots are willing to go to court, if necessary, to confirm what they take to be their basic relationship to the nation. They carry reams of unusual legal briefs.

One system I am aware of in California, which purports to allow a person to redefine his citizenship, and avoid all sorts of dealings with the federal government, includes a bureau which, with a single phone call, intervenes in any sudden "federal problem." A summons has arrived? Advice is given. Specific forms are faxed, to be filled out and sent to fed bureaucrats, and so on.

I am not in a position to evaluate the workability of any of the Sovereign programs. But Sovereign Citizenship tries to give a person a formal way to withdraw his support for Washington. An increasing number of Americans are taking this route as a way of expressing, forcefully, their opinion of government practices which, they feel, contravene the meaning of the Constitution. These people are also making a statement about out-of-control intrusive government agencies, among them the FDA, ATF, and CIA. A number of Patriots I have spoken with, far from being knee-jerk far-right conservatives, are well aware of CIA activities around the world which have killed the sovereignty of other nations. These Patriots do not define American foreign policy as whatever gives our country more power. They would, in fact, like to see the abolition of the CIA as a terminally corrupt entity, which places them way ahead of many liberals on this issue.

While a lot of Patriots have what I would call a MAJOR blind spot when it comes to environmental concerns, younger people coming into the movement are more educated on the subject. We'll see.

At any rate, these people represent a distinct and massively growing threat to Washington-power, to the always-present federal desire to maintain what turns out to be corrupt control of the citizenry.

THE FOURTEENTH IMAGE

Some researchers say that McVeigh, on his own, was planning a disturbance on April 19th. They say that ATF or FBI caught wind of this early on and, hoping for a last-minute glorious arrest, watched him from a distance. Set him up for a sting by encouraging his actions, even helping him. That somewhere along the line they blew it. A last-minute bust never took place. McVeigh wandered away from their lax surveillance and committed the atrocity at the Federal Building. It was a sting that went bad.

I would point out this:

The truck bomb gave off no soot, very little unexploded fertilizer. That's professional. Not McVeigh. The best explanation of that is, a pro rigged a very small ANFO explosion to intentionally leave a bit of fertilizer, to tie McVeigh in. After all, the FBI says it has McVeigh's fingerprint on the receipt for the fertilizer purchase.

Perhaps better yet, the pro doesn't rig a tiny ANFO explosion at all. He just sets up the solid, reliable, non-ANFO charge in the truck which will make a very big bang and take out part of the front wall of the Fed Bldg. He has a bit of fertilizer in the truck, and that will scatter around near the scene and be found by FBI.

Based on this scenario, McVeigh is actually being run by pros, unknown to him. This would not reduce down to a sting gone bad. This would not basically be tragic negligence on the part of federal law enforcement, who lost track of a lone killer at the last moment. This would be a pro who fully intended to set off a bomb. This would be a pro who kept McVeigh in the dark about what was in the back of the truck. This would be other pros who set bombs on columns inside the Murrah Building. This would later become a big-time person(s) distorting an entire FBI investigation. This would be, at the highest level, intentional murder.

THE FIFTEENTH IMAGE

"The overriding issue is national security, because if there isn't any country, then there isn't any jury system."
"But if a man can't get a fair trial, the country is wiped out already."
"Really now, sir. That's sheer hyperbole."
"It isn't."
"You see, if we begin to introduce the possibility that bombs were placed inside the building, then the FBI will be seen to be lying."
"Yes?"
"That's not permitted."
"But the FBI works for the people."
"And who do the people work for?"
"Themselves."
"Nonsense. They work for a higher ideal. One that is embodied in their republic, in their government, in their Constitution, in the men who make up their government. Now, if you allow people to run rampant over those men, over that government, you have nothing left but chaos. I won't be a party to that."
"It appears to me that if federal prosecutors--the federal government--went into a bar and pulled out the drunkest man there, shaved him, gave him a shower, put new clothes on him, and called him to the stand as an expert on bombs and explosions, the court would allow him to testify, would even grant him

deference."
"Yes, that's exactly what I'm implying. Whatever the government chooses is automatically conferred a certain status."
"You're asserting that the government cannot go on trial."
"We have to pay respect to those who have righteousness.
"How did they attain that?"
"Righteousness is not attained. It is exercised as a power. You see, there is a power to define things and words, from the beginning. To make the assumptions and descriptions."
"For oneself, your Honor. Only for oneself."
"Oh no. For others. For everyone. That's your mistake. That's what you don't understand."

EPILOGUE

Whenever you have a large event that contains a mystery, everyone shows up with his favorite explanation. This explanation not only covers the event but many other unrelated happenstances as well. And there is ordinarily a special enemy wheeled in. I don't say this as a heavy criticism, because some of those enemies are real. But in, for example, the case of Oklahoma City, do they count? Are they involved?

Many people will not accept the explanation of an event unless it accuses their favorite target.

"If it isn't the Militias, forget it."
"It's the CIA."
"The Queen of England."
"The Commies are back."
"The Christian far right."
"KKK."
"Liberals."
"Illuminati."
"Rockefeller."

In the case of Oklahoma City, there are people who feel that "McVeigh and his racist militia friends" must be blamed all the way into the center of the conspiracy. Why? Because coming up with any other explanation "lets those bastards off the hook." So left-leaning commentators, who are usually wary of government Bill of Rights abuses and trumped up lies out of Washington, suddenly, for one shining moment, see the government as good. "They have the story absolutely right. The FBI are on the case. They've nailed those racist pigs. I always did like the Bureau." Just remember this. If a dozen free-lance reporters and a million or so free-lance citizens can see all the way through the official scenario about the explosion itself, can see how full of absolute nonsense it is, then so can the FBI. And if the agency in charge of coming up with the truth, the FBI, does not see and does not say what really happened, then that is no accident. That is willful.

Willful has reasons.

At moments like this, people show you where they are on the issue of the federal government itself.

"You see, Washington is all right, it's just that so many Congressmen have breakfast with Pat Robertson. If it weren't for him, things would run well."

"The feds are okay. But some of the Pentagon generals are tied into end-of-the-worlders. You know, those Armageddon types. Otherwise the Army would be a good thing, actually."

"Just give the FBI laser weapons. And microwave guns. They'd fix the criminals. Then the streets would be safe."

"It's not the Pentagon with its twelve billion weapons that's a threat, it's ONLY those Militia people with their semi-assault rifles."

"The problem is, government isn't big enough. If we could just get all the nations of the world together, and make one huge government, our problems would be over. Then all those conniving officials would become compassionate."

"The government doesn't have a basic desire to steamroll the Bill of Rights. We just need to get Clinton Bush Reagan Carter Ford Nixon Johnson

Kennedy Eisenhower Truman Roosevelt Hoover out of the White House in '96..."

An assessment of future federal government? More intrusion locally, nationally, globally. Always intrusion. The attempted marriage of hi-tech and politics, with the mission of a surprising amount of psychological control over the citizenry. The continued trashing of Third World countries, resulting in further availability of land for transnational corporate use. The coalescence of the US military, intelligence agencies, fed law enforcement bureaus, local police into a linked Keeper of the Rules. The continued growth of transnational corporate ant colonies, demanding high-level unthinking loyalty from its workforce.

These scenarios are not surprising. They follow the desires of people who now control government:

The corporate/political/military/ types who, under no circumstances, will ever voluntarily give up power, elections or no elections, Demo or Rep, it matters not. WILL NEVER VOLUNTARILY GIVE UP POWER. And in case you hadn't really thought about it, that is a problem.

Meanwhile, the overwhelming percentage of well-intentioned activist groups in America are trying to REFORM the government.

But a different way is surfacing. Which is the withdrawal of support, across the board, for a terminally destructive federal/corporate organism that, from a base inside the Beltway, is trying to gobble up MORE.

Washington does not realize how many Americans see it this way.

Like a television network which refuses to air the truth, Washington keeps applying more spin, more disinformation, to cover its ant-colony-building activities.
"We're still fooling everyone."
No.
The charade is coming to a close.
The propaganda wings are outflanked.

Jon Rappoport is the author of **AIDS INC.**, **Kill the Monster**, and the editor/author of **U.S. Government Mind Control Experiments on Children**. An investigative report for fifteen years, he hosts the weekly Free Form Radio on KPFK-FM in Los Angeles.

www.ingramcontent.com/pod-product-compliance
Lightning Source LLC
Chambersburg PA
CBHW070647050426
42451CB00008B/302